A Journey Into Being

Knowing and Nurturing Our Children as Spirit

by Christine Ramos, RN, BSN, CCE, CD

OZARK MOUNTAIN PUBLISHING

PO Box 754
Huntsville, AR 72740
www.ozarkmt.com

©Copyright 2006 Christine Ramos

All rights reserved. No part of this book, in part or in whole, may be reproduced, transmitted or utilized in any form or by any means, electronic, photographic or mechanical, including photocopying, recording, or by any information storage and retrieval system without permission in writing from Ozark Mountain Publishing, Inc., except for brief quotations embodied in literary articles and reviews.

For permission, or serialization, condensation, adaptions, or for catalog of other publications, write to: Ozark Mountain Publishing, Inc., PO Box 754, Huntsville, AR 72740, Attn: Permissions Department.

Library of Congress Cataloging-in-Publication Data
Ramos, Christine - 1967 -
"A Journey Into Being" Christine Ramos, RN, BSN, CCE, CD
A registered nurse takes you where science meets spirituality on the transformational voyage of the soul as it prepares for life, unites with the physical body, and undergoes birth.
1. Parenting   2. Metaphysics   3. Child-rearing 4. Pregnancy
I. Ramos, Christine, 1967 -   II. Title

Library of Congress Catalog Number: 2006926237
ISBN: 1-886940-94-0

Cover Art and Layout by www.enki3d.com
Special thanks to Jyn Meyer (jynmeyer.com) for use of her "Pregnancy Yoga" photo that was incorporated into the artwork.
Book Design: Julia Degan
Book Set in: Times New Roman, Asrafel

Published by

PO Box 754
Huntsville, AR 72740

www.ozarkmt.com
Printed in the United States of America

Acknowledgements

To my children Brandon, Ethan, and Emily, who are my sweetest inspiration. Each of you has taught me too much to list here. You have transformed my life and thus my soul by owning the privilege of being your mother. I feel almost unworthy of this rapturous joy you bring me. Thank you for deciding on Dad and I to help guide each of you through this magnificent ride called life. The love I have for each of you transcends spoken words and the limits of time.

To my husband John, who kept the "financial boat" afloat as I had the luxury of writing this book while being a full-time mother for the first time since our first was born years ago. Yes, Honey, you were the one that rescued our first-born from my "expert" parenting. Thank goodness one of us had the sense back then to recognize there is no such expertise. I love you deeply.

To my beloved late mother-in-law "Avó", whose untimely exit from this world placed me at home with my children. Oh, how I wish you could have held your only grand-daughter. To my father-in-law who makes our children the center of his world. Without you all this book would not exist.

And to my family, my mother, my step-father, my sister, and her family, your belief in me gave me the courage to put this all together. I thank and love you all dearly.

Table of Contents

INTRODUCTION

The birth of a every child has the potential to bring a host of powerful thought from the wonderment of creation to the contemplation of things purely philosophical. Questions, both profound and usual, may arise. What is the true purpose of new life? How is it that two siblings reared in the same manner with their biological parents can have such opposite characters? How can we accurately respond to our babies when they cannot tell us what is wrong? Why would our Creator allow a baby to be born just to succumb later to disease? These are some of the mysteries that lie in the heart of just about every parent and person awaiting the arrival of their baby. And the questions are those that fill almost every parenting magazine. *A Journey Into Being* is that book that can address all these and more as it offers an understanding of new life that escapes the scope of science alone. It imparts knowledge of the spirit, that superbly distinct inner being of a child that can bring an individual the deepest love, sweetest wonderment, and most profound grief ever known.

When I was pregnant with my first child I, like most other women, read all the popular books about childbearing during that time. I learned all there was to learn about the anatomy and physiology of pregnancy and childbirth. And my husband and I diligently enrolled in a childbirth education class. I strove to be well prepared for the most momentous event of my life. It paid off. Aside from the fact that I labored only for five hours everything else was anticipated.

But when my second son was conceived things were different for me. Having learned as much as I had and already experiencing pregnancy and childbirth my scope of knowledge was about as complete as I could hope for. Yet I felt something was missing. The sources were aplenty regarding the mechanics of pregnancy, but I found nothing which spoke to the true depth of carrying another life inside me. Nothing that helped justify my overwhelming reverence and guide me through this profoundly spiritual journey that I had the privilege of embarking on.

As a spiritual person and an intuitive I knew enough to understand that nothing is random. Hence I wanted to learn about the *soul* of my unborn child and why I, along with my husband, would be the ones honored to parent him or her. I craved to know the *process* of spirit uniting with physical body. When does it happen and can the mother sense it? Is it possible to communicate with your baby's soul before he/she is born? And could that soul to soul communication carry on into infancy and thereafter? Is it possible to attune with the essence of your child so well that you can actually intuit the inner happenings of your child before she can express them to you?

So I began my search. Having read many works on the subject of spirituality I naturally started there. But all the books I came across mentioned very little, if anything, about what I desired to know regarding a child's journey into life. There were, of course, books on reincarnation, karma, spiritual energies, and newer works on the Indigo Children but nothing on the topic "fundamentals of pregnancy and childbirth, a spiritual perspective", which was essentially what I was looking for.

I began my own quest to put it all together. Applying what I already knew about spirituality allowed me to understand the general concept involved in the coming of new life. And my own intuitive nature gave me basic insight. But the nurse in me demanded empirical evidence of the journey into being. I wanted the support of practical experiences. It meant delving a little deeper to make sound premises backed by available research and reliable observation. However, once I started my search a new reality opened up for me; a spiritual perspective of pregnancy, childbirth, and childrearing that basically brought me to my knees from humility. My research did more than satisfy my curiosity, it completely changed me. What's more, something profound propelled me to share this information despite never having anything published in my name. And now I have gone so far as to write about the subject matter of this book in parenting publications.

Hence, *A Journey Into Being* was created. It will take you where science meets spirituality on the transformational voyage of the soul as it prepares for life, unites with the physical body, and undergoes birth. You will appreciate the process of adaptation to the physical body and world during infancy and childhood. What should then follow is a startling new awareness of a child's soul. Many baffling issues regarding children will subsequently become clear; like why most need to be comforted to sleep and upon awakening. Why some babies suffer from colic, fuss or seem more sensitive than others. What makes them have "feminine" or "masculine" qualities as they grow. Together we will view how an unborn child chooses her family. We will learn how to sense the essence of a child still in utero, how to perceive unorganized energy dynamics in the infant and how to remedy them. We will explore methods for increasing intuitive responsiveness to a child who has yet to learn language; a technique I have termed "Intuitive Nurturing".

One of my greatest hopes for this book is that you may realize the ability to nurture a child's spirit, as well as their mind and body. You will soon see how doing so holds the capacity to promote a child's health, sense of well-being, and thus fulfillment in life. I pray it will offer a new appreciation for that superbly distinct inner being of a child that can bring an individual the deepest love, sweetest wonderment, and most profound grief ever known. I wish also for it to bring you greater awareness as to what new life is really all about. To perhaps look at things differently and find meaning in the seemingly senseless.

Indeed *A Journey Into Being* takes the reader where science meets spirituality. It is a marriage of the worldly facts regarding pregnancy, birth, and childhood with the spiritual truths on which they are founded. Laced throughout the text are medical and nursing research data which supports each premise the book presents. The reader should expect even more confirmations concerning the subject matter in this book as humans continue to spiritually evolve and science further investigates evidence of our everlasting soul.

A Journey Into Being is my tribute to every precious child; for unto this world each brings the power of love and the promise of change... for you, for me, for all creation.

PART ONE

OUR TIMELESS AND ETERNAL ESSENCE

Chapter One

Awakening of the Spirit

"Birthing is the most profound initiation to spirituality a woman can have."

Robin Lim

I believe we are now in an exciting time of change. People from all walks of life in our society are starting to realize that there is so much more to us humans than what meets the eye. The body seems to encompass more than just organized biological material. It contains a radiant energy, that which is the most important part of our being, in other words, our soul, our spirit, our essence. It has the power to heal us and to ail us. It is who we are *before* nature and nurture has a chance to influence our person. For an infant it is the character immediately present after birth like his tranquil and serene disposition, her excited interest in her new world, or his tendency to be unusually fearful. It is the sparkling light within the eyes of a child, the distinctive presence that can fill a room no matter how small the body. It is the timeless and eternal essence, the part of us that transcends all in the physical world.

The spirit is what drives a child's innate passions like a love for dancing, a gift of artistry, or talent for leadership. It is how two brothers can have completely opposite characters although raised in the same manner by the same parents. By the same token, innateness is the distinct similarities shared between siblings who were reared separately, because their souls are eternal companions. Science cannot explain innateness in an individual because it is the expression of the soul. There are no genetic codes that can reflect nor predict the traits the soul brings with it when personified. Certain strengths and weaknesses in a young child are the inherent traits of that child's essence. The child comes into this world not as a clean slate, but as an everlasting soul born to fulfill its divine purpose. He has an agenda for his life, and although intermingled with the lives of its chosen family its soul is not a reflection of those he physically resembles. He may have the same color eyes as his mother, the same feet as his father, and the same wavy hair as his brother, but know that a child's soul is purely unique. Conception is just part of the continuum of a soul's existence, the journey into emerging greatness.

As time moves forward more of us are starting to accept the concept of the human spirit as an integral part of our existence, regardless of our religion. People are sensing the need for and actively seeking a lifestyle that addresses the holism of the self. Spirituality is flourishing and unlike religion it is more expansive, capable of enriching a person's life through nature, art, music, exercise, and even scientific thought. Consciousness is being recognized as the presence of the soul, the essence of the body.

I think the emergence of so many gifted and courageous intuitives in publication and the media are a positive indication of our changing mindset. Numerous publications are being written about the spirit, and not just by mystics. Persons of all religious backgrounds and educational levels, including those who hold doctorate degrees, are writing books and articles of spiritual nature. Subjects ranging from meditation and cardiac disease to the power of prayer have been and continue to be published. In fact the topic is now quite mainstream. Yoga and t'ai chi, both based on ancient spiritual practices, are now very popular forms of exercise. Recognized for its effectiveness in somehow transcending the sole goal of just physical fitness, devotees swear by their holistically therapeutic benefits and claim improved quality of living.

The healthcare system too is taking notice. Providers are now recognizing that in order for true healing to occur we must address mind, body, *and soul*. Healthcare journals are loaded with new information on the effectiveness of treating disease with both traditional and complimentary treatments. Methods such as acupuncture, massage therapy, and Reiki, all of which influence the flow of subtle human energy, are being acknowledged as restorative approaches to health. One recent study cites spirituality as the cause for improved quality of life in those with life threatening illness. These people were less depressed and better able to cope with their situation compared with their non-spiritual counterparts. Another groundbreaking study conducted at Duke University has recently confirmed that prayer may in fact help heal a person. Prayer, simply put, is healing energy for the spirit; healing energy for yourself or to send to someone through compassionate intentions.

Currently there are several pioneering hospitals across the nation that have implemented holistic programs which focus on connecting mind, body, and spirit as part of helping patients prepare for surgery and/or recover their health. These programs have been shown to impressively improve patient outcomes. Some of the major health insurance companies are even covering the costs for the various services I have mentioned. Will orthodox medicine someday routinely consider the role of the spirit in its delivery of care? In light of what has proven effective in restoring and maintaining health thus far, it may not have a choice.

Let us consider for instance those awe-inspiring Near Death Experiences where persons who were clinically dead and moments later revived recount similar happenings, including seeing a glorious light and/or deceased loved ones meeting them on the "other side". Nursing journals have recently educated the nursing profession on how to care for these individuals who have experienced NDEs. Specifically, we are instructed not to touch the top of their head as, according to study, this seems to be the sacred area where the spirit departs. Any physical contact in that area can deeply upset the patient and should be avoided. Then there are those who have been in a state of unconsciousness who, when they awaken, can accurately describe events which occurred during their unconscious state. There have been confirmed reports of these patients having detailed knowledge of conversations between healthcare personnel which occurred *outside* of their room.

And what about those mysteries conjoined twins present to the medical community? Specifically, twins joined at the skull who share frontal lobe tissue of the brain. These siblings are shown to possess totally separate personalities. Yet how can this be so if the frontal lobe is what controls a person's attitude, affect, judgment, and behavior; all things which make up individuality? How can two physical bodies sharing the largest portion of the brain, the part that shapes personality, have two very distinct characters? Simple. When it is the intended journey toward the spiritual growth of two *individual* souls. Mystifying yes, however only to those who view our existence within the confines and limitations of what can be observed, measured, and explained in physical terms.

Applying New Awareness to the Upbringing of Our Children

New life beholds all that is authentic of the soul. Not yet tainted by life experiences, an infant may present behaviors which seem curious if not down right challenging. Why do most babies need to be comforted to sleep and upon awakening? Why is it that some fuss, have colic, or seem more sensitive than others. How is it that even identical twin newborns can clearly have different temperaments when they share the same genetic composition? I

6

can go on and on. Indeed these are some of the mysteries that lie in the heart of just about every person who has or will have a child. And the questions are those that fill almost every parenting magazine. Yet the answers are not as accessible as reaching for a journal of expertise, nor are they as universal as any scholar can profess. The answers are those which lie in that same domain, that of the spirit.

And again, as trends reflect the importance of achieving that fulfillment of inner life, we are seeing a change within the basic foundation of family life. For example, more working mothers are opting to stay at home to raise their children if they have the option to do so. According to a March 2004 *Time Magazine* article, the proportion of working, married, mothers with children under age 3 dropped from 61% in 1997 to 58% in 2002. And I believe their decision to leave the workforce, or to seek part-time jobs to be more involved in the raising of their children, involves more than just the realization of needing more balance in their lives. I suspect that women are also being intuitively drawn to their own spiritual needs as a mother as well as that of her children's.

Furthermore, as we look to fulfill our inner lives, as individuals and as parents, one of the questions that arises is whether there is anything we have been missing when it comes to our children's healthy upbringing. We now know of the various spiritual practices and perspectives available for our benefit. Just pick up any mainstream magazine and you are bound to read something on the many topics regarding some form of spirituality. But what can we do for our children to ensure that we are giving them the unsurpassed benefits that spirituality imparts? Moreover, are we adequately nurturing *their souls* as well as their bodies and minds? Might their needs be slightly different than ours because of their newness to life? These are the questions I wish address in this book for I believe there is an immediate need for guidance, for parents as well as anyone else who has a child in their lives.

Therefore I am very thrilled about these changes in trend for they are starting to put an emphasis on things we have ignored for too long; like how to attend to the inner being of infants and older children in a world so consumed by our own hurried pace. Just think about all the advancements we have made in this society and how it has bred a faster paced population who expect immediate results and gratification. Things rightfully reserved for natural processes are no longer. Everything, from the food that nourishes us to the way we usher in new life, has been colored by the illusion of what apparently is convenient, cost effective, and efficient, must be better for us. We have lost sight of nature and God's course of creation. All for the sake of keeping up with the pace that our society has produced.

Indeed we still have a long way to go when it comes to knowing our children as spirit. It is time that we finally provide them with an upbringing that nurtures their entire being, for they indeed have special needs and challenges. I believe that an unfortunate side effect of these intellectual advancements is that we have surrendered our natural intuitiveness as parents guiding our children. We look to the authors of parenting advice books, our pediatricians, or our educators, etc., to provide us with advice no matter how unique our child is. So we abandon our intuitive bond with our children, we quiet the little voice inside ourselves that tells us exactly what's going on with our beloveds. We no longer trust our own instincts when it comes to our children's spirits. Or when we do try to voice our intuitive knowledge of our children we oftentimes succumb to the advice of those who purport to know otherwise. As a nurse, I cannot tell you how many times I have heard that a mother knew exactly what was wrong with her sick child before she entered her pediatrician's office. Most times, of course, the practitioner confirms what they instinctively knew was wrong with their child. However, I also know of times when the practitioner misses the proper diagnosis, and parent and child are sent home only to return several days later. When asked, the parent will usually admit that they somehow sensed the misdiagnosis from the beginning. As a parent there have been many times I have brought my child in to the pediatrician's office with an *impending* illness that needed treatment. Not because of any symptoms but rather because of an intuitive sense about a slight change in my child's disposition.

From the moment they are born there are struggles unique to a young child that a mature, "adapted" adult simply just does not endure. For example: Have you ever wondered why babies need so much comforting to go to sleep, and at times upon awakening? It is such a frustrating perplexity in our society that volumes of books have been written about it and parenting magazines are swamped with advice about "How to Get Your Baby to Sleep". Have you ever noticed how a newborn may cry while being held by a family member, but will immediately calm down in the arms of his mother? I assure you it is more than her scent he is sensing. Have you ever marveled at how a premature baby experiences increased growth, and immune function leading to an earlier hospital discharge, all because she was placed on her mother's chest periodically throughout the day? And when twins share the same bed, the health of the weaker of the two improves simply by being close to his sibling?

The fact is that none of these phenomena can be explained entirely by mere science, for these are the subtle yet powerful nuances of the everlasting soul. All children, from newborn to young adulthood share this exceptionally vulnerable period of transformation; although it may simply be a question of to what degree. This period is a time of adjustment, when the consciousness of a spiritual being must adapt to the new experiences of physical embodiment. Our baby was once a being of fine vibratory matter, and has an amazing undertaking ahead of her. As an infant she must master the task of organizing, directing, and conserving her energies so that her new body can function the way it is supposed to. This includes regulating her breathing and heart rates, her digestive system, and her sleep/wake cycles. And as she continues to grow she must face the elusive task of integrating her spiritual consciousness with the workings of her biological mind and body. An often lifetime endeavor; I call this event of maturation "Mind-Body-Soul Integration", an alignment of spirit consciousness with the flesh. As you might have guessed on your own, those children who achieve a complete integration will undoubtedly grow to lead fulfilled lives, regardless of what their society deems as being successful. More on this in subsequent chapters.

Some children enter our world and adapt without much difficulty, these are the hearty ones. Souls that do not require a lot of assistance in adapting to our physical reality. These are what some may call the "easy" or "good" babies. The ones who can sleep through the night without a peep, they do not fuss a lot, and seem to always be in a passive mood, undisturbed by the world around them . Then there are the children who have some difficulty adapting to physical life. These are the sensitive and soulful babies. They are the children who need plenty of assistance. The fussy ones, the ones who will experience colic, and severe separation and stranger anxiety. As older children they may be emotionally sensitive, or perhaps still need assistance in some capacity.

Because of their difficulties they may present those around them with special challenges, in terms of their education and socialization. These children may respond negatively to some traditional approaches to parenting and education. Providing discipline and guidance seems to only be effective if carried out with the utmost love and affection. These children cannot be "trained" to go to sleep, nor will they positively react to any type of detached instruction. These are the children, because of their challenges, that are changing the way we as adults view parenting, healthcare, and education. These are the children who are prompting us to question hospital practices that separate parent and child for no logical reason. These are the kids who are forcing us to look at what is and is not working for them in terms of learning academically. These are the kids who, because of their challenges, are bringing us back to what is really important, matters and needs of the soul.

In this book, I will also introduce you to a concept I have termed "Intuitive Nurturing" which involves strategies to help us know our children as spirit. I will be covering these strategies in detail. So what exactly is this book about? I will begin by first telling you what it is not. *A Journey Into Being* is not your typical parenting advice book, for I believe every child deserves much more than being grouped into a general approach toward child rearing. You will not hear me instruct you on the best way to raise our children, because I believe no one can be an expert on the complexity that comprises an individual soul. What works for one child may not for even his sibling. *A Journey Into Being* is a thought provoking piece specifically intended to encourage all people who have children in their lives, to take notice of their distinct inner beings. The part of them that is timeless and as such has a history. And a future whose purpose is to strive for the progression of themselves, as well as for those they share that time and space with. Our role in their life as primarily being a catalyst for them. It is intended to help you realize the phenomenal journey to physical life. To appreciate a child's unique challenges during Mind-Body-Soul Integration and to provide the awareness needed to assist them through it. Most importantly *A Journey Into Being* will give you the practical understanding needed to view a child's *soul,* thus facilitating an approach to parenting (as well as other roles) that is right for that particular child. My method of doing this is not by direct instruction, for again our children are too exceptional for that. My method instead is to have you revisit the spiritual journey to physical life. A journey no doubt veiled from your waking consciousness. I wish to immerse you in the worlds before our first breath and thereafter. There is where the answers to many questions will appear regarding the true purpose of new life and why those puzzling childhood happenings occur.

We will follow the creation and development of new life from preconception through childhood. Again, I will take you into the realm of the spirit where you can behold the existence of the essence *before* its physical birth. I will present to you the very complex process of incarnation and how, during pregnancy, the spirit unites with the physical body. I will instruct you on how to intuitively sense and communicate with the essence of a child both before and after birth. "Intuitive nurturing" is intended to promote a relationship with your children that includes increased responsiveness to their unspoken needs. It is a process of utilizing methods that help you to know the child's distinct spirit. Methods that have been unequivocally shown to increase parental awareness and sensitivity. And by truly knowing the strengths and weaknesses of the inner being of a child your responsiveness to their individual needs is far more effective and compassionate than *any* child rearing manual can advise. I will show you how to gently welcome the newly incarnated spirit into the world while providing the infant with very basic spiritual needs. As we examine the unique energy patterns of the infant, and later the child, those common childhood occurrences shall be explained. Prior child-rearing tactics will be found insensitive and actually damaging to the healthy development of the soul, thus possibly affecting the physical body as the child ages. All the while I will be presenting the most recent medical and nursing research data that will support each of my premises.

You will find in the first half of this book I will be working on creating a framework which will serve as the foundation in the spiritual understanding of a child's journey into being. Part of that framework will be the presentation of the anatomical structure of the human energy field. While we explore it you will discover how dysfunctional energy patterns of the body arise and how they can lead to illness, for it is the spirit which sustains the physical body through the delicate balance between

12

mind, body, and spirit. More specifically, you shall be made aware of how spiritually repressive beliefs and attitudes can alter the vibrational workings of the spirit. And how an adult's perspective can easily influence the well-being of our children in a most negative way.

One of my hopes for this book is that after reading it you may see the larger picture and experience the deeper meaning of many situations in life. I guess you could say I wish to alter your perception of life. I will encourage you to challenge your current thoughts and perceptions about what it means to live a fulfilled existence, for it is this achievement we wish for our children. I will ask you to ponder your own upbringing and examine how it has shaped who you are now, and how that may influence the manner in which you nurture a child in your life.

Working in the social service field, then later as a nurse caring for adults, pregnant women, and children provided me with the fascinating experience of witnessing the dynamics and interconnection between mind, body, and soul. The experience imparted precious awareness of the importance of addressing the unique needs of our children in a truly holistic manner. The lessons are invaluable. I am confident that once we truly understand and nurture the essence of a child we will raise a generation of empathic, sensitive, and intuitive individuals who can lead the way to a harmonious existence in a better, healthier world. *A Journey Into Being* is about empowering you with that awareness of how to bring out the uniquely magnificent brilliance within the bodies of each and every young one.

My goal is to continually unite science with spirituality throughout this book. I will take you on a spiritual, and corresponding physical, journey into being, starting from preconception. Together we will examine a type of nurturing for our children that is medically unexplainable, yet spiritually sensible in terms of why they are so effective in aiding their healthy growth and development. Components of this approach include the lovely practices of Kangaroo Care, co-bedding, infant massage, Therapeutic Touch, and "wearing" your child in a carrier device, all of which include an additional benefit of promoting intuitive nurturing. The studies on the benefits of these practices are out there. However, it is only with knowledge of the spirit that their curious effectiveness can be explained.

Without further delay, let us embark on this wondrous trip by introducing you to the basic concept of the human energy field. In the following chapter we will examine the two core energy dynamics which compose the human spirit: the vibrational layers and chakra system. Some of the information is general, so feel free to skim over what you are already familiar with.

Chapter Two

Spirit Anatomy 101

"To exist is to change, to change is to mature, to mature is to go on creating oneself endlessly."

Henri Bergson

Early on in my nursing career when I worked on a cardiac unit, I had my first tangible experience with the departure of the human essence from the physical body. I began my shift one day as usual, taking report on my assigned patients from the night nurse. The nurse informed me that one of my patients was a 71 year old man who had been in a state of unconsciousness since having a stroke about a week before. He was transferred to our floor from ICU after the insertion of a pacemaker and was expected to slowly increase his responsiveness to stimuli, as he had recently made some improvements. I made a note to perform a thorough neurological assessment for this patient and went out to make my morning rounds.

However, when I met Mr. B. I instantly *sensed* something very different from the gradual improvement I was told to expect. I immediately checked his cardiac monitor to see if there were any abnormalities in his heart rate or rhythm, but there were none. When I returned to his bedside, and after performing a thorough physical assessment, I noted that he was in the same physical condition as the night nurse reported to me. So what was it that I sensed? When I focused in on my perceptions I realized a certain inconsistent, dull, erratic, and slow moving energy flowing through my patient. I felt this energy through every part

15

of me as I performed my nursing assessment and while I provided his care. My entire being simply *knew* his soul was in the process of departing from his physical body, although there were no clinical signs. My patient remained the same throughout the course of my shift. But when I gave report to the night nurse after my shift I told her that I suspected Mr. B. would not live much longer, and to be mindful of his DNR order, (Do Not Resuscitate). She, of course, asked for clinical justification of my remark, of which I could not give her. When I returned to work the next morning the night nurse reported that Mr. B. indeed passed on that late evening. She asked me how was I able to tell that he was about to die, and all I could say was that I just felt a certain dreadful "vibe" coming from him. Since then, whenever that particular nurse took report from me, she would ask, "So Christine, do any of these patients have that "death vibe" going on? Because if so, I'll just park the *Crash Cart outside their room". (*A special cart stocked with life saving equipment and medications used in the event of cardiac arrest or other life threatening emergency.)

THOSE GOOD VIBRATIONS

Science has known for centuries that living tissue generates energy. Consider for a moment how our very own heart beats: an electrical conduction system causes the cardiac muscle to contract and relax. A fact which led to the invention of the electrocardiogram in 1902. Our brain and nervous systems function by sending electrical impulses throughout our body; a physiological system we can now quite easily record through the use of electroencephalogram (EEG). Even our DNA has been measured to vibrate with energy at a rate of 52 to 78 gigahertz (billions of cycles per second.).

All in nature is made of energy; humans, of course, being the most complex. The Earth too resonates with it. Along with the

Sun they produce a life supporting essence called the "universal energy". Universal energy is that which sustains all of creation on this planet. It is what nourishes and promotes the growth of *all* living organisms including plants, animals, humans, and one celled life forms like bacteria and fungi.

On the scientific front, quantum physics concur that there is a vibratory essence in every living being. In the early 1900's physicist Albert Einstein proved that matter and energy are in fact the same thing, simply expressed in two different forms. Laws of energy state that energy itself cannot be created or destroyed, instead it simply transforms. The dense physical body follows the laws of bioenergetics and thermodynamics in that all living cells in the body use then lose energy to the environment each time it carries out its biological task. As the biological system runs down and subsequently dies that energy which sustained its vital functions is released into the environment. Matter is transformed into a higher, finer vibratory form of energy, about the same as that of light. This is the nature of energy as it exists in our physical world.

So where exactly does all that organized energy go when the physical body meets its demise? According to science and its laws of energy it is not extinguished or lost. According to friends and family of loved ones passed on, the unmistakable presence of their beloved is at times felt throughout their lives. Indeed, the vibratory essence of our physical being transcends that which has limits of time and space; it is eternal, it is our spirit. And while beliefs regarding the existence of the soul may vary greatly from one individual to the other, there is one thing I am sure we can all agree upon, the human being is so much more than just an organized structure of living cells. Poetically termed as the windows to the soul, the eyes display a radiance behind them; the body containing a palpable vibrancy so distinctly absent when there is death.

Most of what we know regarding the energy dynamics of the human spirit is taken from knowledge of the Far East and

India where the soul is recognized as the fundamental part of a living being. And indeed it is. So essential is our soul that it is able to influence the health of our physical body. A fact which I believe will be accepted and better understood within the medical community in the not-so-distant future. It is becoming impossible to continue ignoring the role of the spirit and the benefits of having a spiritual perspective, as Western science has done all these years. More and more studies are revealing the power of the human spirit, from achieving healing through prayer to alleviating pain by rebalancing spiritual energy through acupuncture. Understanding the nature of our spiritual existence is vital to our own evolution; it is time we all look beyond the material and see the one thing that promises eternity, our and our children's glorious souls.

The following is a crash course in the fundamentals of spirit anatomy. It is basic information on the human energy field which will serve as the foundation for exploring how the energy dynamics of the newly incarnated spirit is unique, and why it is so important to understand in terms of addressing the needs of a child. It is also presented to provoke reflective thought on the dynamics of your own soul, and how they may affect a child you have influence upon. Again, if this is familiar to you, simply skim through it.

As I have said already many times, our eternal and timeless spirit is composed of vibrational matter; it swirls, pulsates in, around and through our bodies nourishing each and every cell with vibrant energy. There are two dynamics involved:

(1) Layers of energy extending beyond the physical body.

(2) Vortices of energy, called chakras, lined up vertically along the center of your body which influence the layers.

Front aspect of chakras and layers of energy.

Side aspects of chakras funneling energy into its spiritual, and consequently, its physical bodies.

Layers

As shown in the illustration there are four major layers or bodies extending from our physical body like energy templates. Each layer, starting with the physical body as the densest part, is comprised of vibrating life energy fields of increasingly higher and finer levels of energy and matter. The color and intensity of our layers are largely dependent on the health and happenings of the energy centers of the chakras. This is what makes up the field of our aura.

Etheric layer: This is the layer closest to our physical body and the one that most resembles it. Our etheric layer is a mass of energy which serves as a template onto which the cells of a developing fetus organize. Have you ever wondered how a fertilized egg "knows" how to differentiate itself into such a complex structure as a human being? Embryonic development remains a mystery to researchers. The etheric layer of our essence serves as a guide for physical growth, from conception to adulthood. When we experience bodily injury this network of energy aids in the regeneration of damaged cells needed to heal.

Consider for a moment the phantom limb phenomenon. People who have had a limb amputated often report feeling sensations in the area where their limb once was. They may experience pain, itching, pressure, and temperature as though their limb still existed. As a registered nurse, I have worked with such individuals, and believe me, these sensations are very real. So much so that emotional support and sometimes various medications are often needed to help them cope. To date there is no medical explanation for this phenomenon. But what does make sense is that regardless of amputation our etheric body remains intact, thereby providing an invisible structure of what once was.

A dramatic example of the function of the etheric layer can be seen in the cellular repair of a salamander's body when

21

A Journey Into Being

injured. This animal can amazingly regenerate parts of its body which have been removed, such as its leg, tail, ear, and even an eye! Studies have shown that even when the developing cells of tail were removed and placed on the stump of a leg, a leg grew, not a tail. Logically, if the DNA code of a cell tells it to grow a tail then it should grow a tail regardless of where the cells are located. This baffles scientists. Subsequently, researchers agree that there must be a sort of higher intelligence or "morphogenic" field which changes the order of the cell. Hence the scientific correlation with the spiritual etheric field.

Emotional layer: This is the second layer which extends two to four inches away from the physical body. It contains your emotions, both positive and negative. Positive emotions such as joy, love, and hope create a radiant field of energy while negative emotions like fear, anger, or shame cause an erratic, or sometimes incomplete field.

If you are like most people you can sense when someone is angry. Much more than just seeing the person's body language we can sometimes actually feel a thick, pushing, or spiky sensation. Think about the phrase "the air was so thick, you could cut it with a knife", often used to describe a situation involving angry individuals. I myself get off-balanced when I am around someone who has nervous energy. I become disoriented, unfocused, and exasperated.

On the other hand let's examine how a joyful, loving person makes us feel. Words like radiant, warm, glowing all describe how we perceive such a person. Positive emotions promote health by bathing your physical body with radiant energy. Negative emotions promote disease by creating energy leaks, stagnation, and blockages.

Mental layer: This body of energy, which emanates four to eight inches away from us, holds our intellect, our thoughts, our ideas, and our mental processes. It also holds our beliefs and attitudes. This field of energy expands when we are in deep concentration. Clairvoyant people who can perceive human energies say that thoughts can appear in this field as symbolic images.

The mental layer of our being reflects the perception and understanding of our world from our five senses. In our society this seems to be a dominant energy of our being. Reality is interpreted through what is tangible. If you cannot see it, smell it, touch it, hear it, or taste it, it simply does not exist. Long abandoned is intuition and the wisdom of the spirit.

Astral layer: Radiating eight to twelve inches from our physical body is the astral layer, a glorious part of our essence which serves as a bridge between our physical and spiritual realms. It is a portion of ourselves that contains a higher awareness, the part of our spirit which knows the purpose of our present incarnation. You see, we as eternal beings utilize human experience and choice for the purpose of spiritual growth. Somewhere within your higher awareness is the knowledge of your sacred plan, what your spirit has agreed to experience in this lifetime for its divine development. The astral layer of our essence contains this knowledge, and as such, it knows where it has been and where it *should* be going.

Our higher self remembers its timeless existence; it does not undergo "incarnate amnesia", the absence of past life memory. Have you ever met someone or been in a situation which felt strangely familiar to you? Like the co-author of a screenplay your higher self is recognizing a scene from a script it has helped to write. This is momentary access to the awareness of your astral energy; perhaps an affirmation that you are at present following your chosen spiritual path.

Unfortunately, because we now live in an time where man predominantly uses intellect and so little intuition in their lives, this divine knowledge is often forsaken. We are taught at an early age to ignore or rationalize any information perceived outside the five senses. Terms such as "psychic", "extrasensory perception" (ESP), or "paranormal" have developed negative connotations. Perhaps this is due to the emergence of inauthentic "psychic services" that have appeared in the media in the past two decades or so which seem to prey on vulnerable individuals. Intuition *is* the ability to tap into the wisdom of our higher selves and to view life through the eyes of the soul.

As incarnate beings we can access our higher selves when the rational mind rests. During sleep it is this level of consciousness which communicates with us by way of symbolic messages through dreams. Those who can meditate at will enter this level of higher awareness and may experience spiritual visions.

The astral layer of our spirit is the body of energy which separates from the physical body when it is in a state of unconsciousness. It is the same level of awareness that, as I mentioned before, can perceive its surroundings although apart from the physical senses of the body.

Chakras

So much has been written about the wondrous but complex system of our chakras, the energy centers of the soul. Consequently, I will try to condense a fraction of that information as it pertains to this book. A chakra (Sanskrit word meaning "wheel") is a vortex of spinning energy. Like a luminous whirlpool it pulls life energy into our bodies. The chakras of our spirit nourish our physical bodies by bathing it with vibratory sustenance.

There are seven major chakras aligned vertically from the base of our spine to the crown of our head. There are also many other smaller chakras throughout the body (in the hands, feet, knees, to name a few), but for the purpose of this book I will only be discussing the seven major energy centers.

Each of the major chakras covers a specific region of the body along with its internal organs. It acts as a receptor that funnels in the subtle Universal energy which surrounds us. The same invisible life force we share with all other living creations, such as animals and plants.

Intrinsic to each chakra is divine knowledge and power. It is the quest of our spirit to realize these divine truths through the use of human experience and choice. What we experience in our lives and the choices we make, including how we perceive those life experiences, are the elements that determine our progress toward spiritual evolution. The chakras can be a reflection of the success, or lack, of our journey. I will be discussing each of these truths in detail in the next part of this book.

A healthy chakra is open and vibrant with a steady clockwise spin. In contrast an unhealthy chakra can be constricted, closed, or overactive, meaning spinning excessively. Depending on these dynamics, the human energy field has the potential to over-stimulate, inhibit, or change the activity of the human cell. This includes direct influence on the secretion of hormones, cell production, and cellular changes during division and replication.

There are various causes of energy distortions; they can be present at birth and/or acquired. Some can be brought upon the physical world from the spiritual for the purpose of working out or correcting an issue, as part of a sacred plan between the individual and our Creator. An example of this may be a physically disabling congenital disorder which encourages the soul toward empowerment and perseverance despite obstacles. Energy imbalances may also emerge through subtle vibratory influences within the environment, like invisible energy waves, and even from other people you are in frequent contact with. More on that later.

But perhaps more than those, during this point in time of our spiritual evolution, energy distortions may be the result of how we personally interpret life issues and challenges. Whatever significant emotional, mental, or spiritual turmoil we choose to internalize and give power to will cause us psychological stress, which then initiates the stress response in our bodies. Imbalance of the spirit in this case originates from energy distortions created by the secular mind. The series of events go like this: the mind, with its inhibiting perspective, initiates imbalance of the spirit, which then causes physiologic changes in the body. These physiologic changes, over time render you vulnerable to the development of illness and disease.

And indeed medical research supports this. Studies are revealing more and more the link between an individual's physical, mental, and emotional reaction to environmental demands or changes and the promotion of disease. It is now believed that 80%-90% of all disease is related to stress and how one copes with it. Stress, generated by both negative and positive occurrences, is a normal part of life, no one can dispute that. The loss of a job, the start of a new one, the death of a loved one can all produce significant stress in one's life. However, it is when we experience excessive and prolonged reactions to events interpreted as stressful that we run into health problems. Physiological responses to stress cause significant imbalance to the systems of the body which can lead to increased risk of infection, problems with metabolism, and digestive illnesses, just to name a few.

But what is it that causes an individual to experience such profound and chronic stress? Is it not how we view life? What makes a difference in the level of stress we experience is not *what* stressor enters our lives but *how* we adapt to that stressor. When one perceives their life as valuable and views life's changes as positive opportunities rather than as threats, that person reduces the power of stress to wreak havoc on the physical body. Not surprising is the fact that persons who possess spiritual faith/belief share this perspective of life and therefore respond with better coping mechanisms to stressors.

How do you perceive your life and the world around you? What children look up to you? Are you that angry mother at the grocery checkout line who loses her composure because the new employee is not as swift as you want her to be? Are you that healthcare practitioner who scoffs when I ask you to address my child's pain? Are you that grandfather who is always complaining about his life and blames God for every misfortune he encounters? Certain life events are placed in our paths for the sole purpose of assisting us in growing spiritually. It may be to help us realize a part of ourselves we are ignoring, or perhaps to provoke a more meaning-centered perspective of life. As many people can attest to, sometimes only tragedy can awaken us into seeing what truly matters in life.

Spiritually erroneous attitudes, beliefs and behaviors that not only stifle our own progression as spiritual beings but may also lay the foundation for a state of unhealthiness developing in *our children*. A child whose mother is always fretful will see her environment as unsafe. A child whose father is filled with hate will view others with contempt. A child whose teacher ignores his special learning needs will grow to think himself as stupid. All of these are obvious examples of how a child can assume negative physical and mental reactions to their environment as a consequence of the adult influence in their lives. But what is not as obvious, is the injury to the harmonious flow of her spirit as well.

Researchers have identified certain disease promoting attitudes, beliefs, and behaviors. These include feeling dependent on others, helplessness, hopelessness, extreme fear or anger, cynicism or distrust of others; and believing you are socially disadvantaged because of your race, gender, educational level, etc.. Remember these as we interrelate with our children. I believe the region of the body where we hold detrimental perceptions of life (as outlined in the following list of chakras), largely determines where disease manifests itself.

Let me give you something else to think about. As the chakras of our body funnel in subtle Universal energy so too can it take in the subtle energies from *another individual*. This is especially so of fragile beings, such as children. I am sure you have heard the advice given many times to parents trying to calm their fussy infant, which is for them to be calm themselves. Why? The widely accepted explanation is because their baby can *sense* when the parent who is holding them is upset. Let us examine this statement further. What exactly is it that the baby is sensing? Muscle tension? It does not seem logical when the only muscles in contact with them are the parent's arms and chest which are naturally flexed while embracing the baby's body. Could it be the tone of the parents voice? Not so when many parents report they are either silent or singing a lullaby when trying to calm their baby. What the baby is sensing is the parent's emotions. She does this by taking in her parent's subtle energies.

Do not underestimate the vibratory influence of another. Keep this in mind with everyone your baby interacts with. Some babies are more sensitive than others. These are the babies who cry when people other than the parents try to hold them, or those who quickly become over-stimulated when well-wishers stop by the house. And no, I am not talking about "stranger anxiety", a time when baby reacts to strangers with fear at around six to nine months of age. Fragile and sensitive babies will react negatively to unfamiliar human energy patterns right from the time they are born, often able to be held and comforted only by one person, usually the mother. Both my second son and my daughter displayed absolute fear and misery whenever certain people tried to hold them during their first six months of life. My daughter, who was more reactive than my son, could only be held and comforted by me. Many friends and family members who visited us told me that when Emily looked at them she appeared to be looking through their eyes into the depths of their soul. After making her obvious assessment, Emily would inevitably reject our visitor. What exactly was it that kept her from getting too close to each person, I will never really know. But what I *do* know is that she perceived something that made her soul uncomfortable, whether that perception was judicious or not.

The following is a list of our chakras with an abbreviated description on what region of the body they nourish, what perceptions may alter their energy flow, and consequentially what disorders may arise. (Again, there are numerous books that provide greater detail if you wish to read up on the subject). And no, I am not implying that we ourselves are exclusively responsible for the development of disease within our physical bodies. I believe there is *no* living human who has knowledge of God's plan for the path of another. However, what I am asking is that you examine your own beliefs, behaviors, and attitudes and see if you discover anything familiar with what is written below. Then consider your influence on a child in your life.

Root Chakra

Part of anatomy it nourishes: Feet, legs, perineum hips, bones, immune system, genitals, anus, male gonads.

Psychosocial and/or spiritual issues: Fear,   apathy, disconnectedness, concern over survival and personal safety, lack of meaning and purpose.

Possible physiological/mental manifestations: Depression, varicosities (varicose veins, hemorrhoids), some immune disorders including arthritis and allergies, substance abuse, and addiction.

Sacral Chakra

Part of anatomy it nourishes: Female gonads, bladder, uterus, rectum, prostate, sigmoid colon, lumbar spine.

Psychosocial and/or spiritual issues: problems with intimacy (including those secondary to rape, incest), sexual promiscuity, problems with one on one relationships, fear of financial loss, lack of creative energy.

Possible physiological/mental manifestations: Chronic urinary tract infections, gynecological infections and disorders, some hormonal disorders, sexual impotency, infertility, cancers within this region, chronic lower back pain.

Solar Plexus

Part of anatomy it nourishes: intestines, liver, stomach, pancreas, adrenals, kidneys, spleen, lower thoracic spine.

Psychosocial and/or spiritual issues: Loss of identity, self respect, self esteem, ego, emotional dependence, easily intimidated, eager to please, powerlessness, mistrusting, need to control external environment.

Possible physiological/mental manifestations: Hypertension, digestive disorders, "colic", obesity, anorexia, bulimia, diabetes, stomach ulcers, intestinal problems, liver and renal disorders, anxiety/depressive disorders, cancers within this region.

Heart Chakra

Part of anatomy it nourishes: Heart, lungs, breasts, diaphragm, circulatory system, thymus, arms, ribs, upper thoracic spine.

Psychosocial and/or spiritual issues: Difficulty loving others, inability to forgive, difficulty loving oneself, lack of nurturing, self-care; hate, lack of compassion and hope.

Possible physiological/mental manifestations: Cardiac disorders, pulmonary disorders, asthma, some immune disorders, allergies, cancers within this region.

Throat Chakra

Part of anatomy it nourishes: Larynx, vocal cords, esophagus, mouth, tongue, teeth, gums, thyroid, parathyroid, cervical spine.

Psychosocial and/or spiritual issues: Difficulty expressing

oneself, problems with asserting oneself, stating one's opinion, lack of personal will, volition, inability to speak one's own mind.
Possible physiological/mental manifestations: Frequent sore throats, tonsillitis, oral lesions, gum disorders, thyroid disorders, cancers of this region.

Brow Chakra

Part of anatomy it nourishes: Eyes, nose, ears, pituitary gland, pineal gland, cerebral function related to all senses except for touch, mental processes (learning, judgment, affect, etc.).
Psychosocial and/or spiritual issues: Difficulty seeing truth, lack of insight, denial, narrow and close mindedness.
Possible physiological/mental manifestations: Chronic headaches, migraine, ongoing addictions, vision problems, sinus problems, middle and inner ear disorders and infections, learning disabilities, difficulty processing and remembering information, cancers within this region.

Crown Chakra

Part of anatomy it nourishes: Cerebral function related to the *interpretation* of physical reality: skin perceptions- heat, pressure, pain, etc.; motor perceptions- proprioception, body position, sense of space; visual, auditory.
Psychosocial and/or spiritual issues: Feelings of spiritual injustice, blame and anger at God for life's adversities, abandonment of religion or spirituality, fixation on earthly possessions.
(Note: Upon physical death, a soul with the above Crown issues may remain earthbound as a result of avoiding the afterlife either because of not accepting its immortal state or refusing to leave behind its earthly possessions.)

Possible physiological/mental manifestations: Mental illness, multi-organ failure, severe skin disorders, muscular disorders, neurological disorders.

The next chapter, I present to you as food for thought. It is intended to provoke contemplation when considering the source and development of disease. I have specifically chosen to explore these particular diseases as they usually arise in childhood, and the medical community has already suggested a significant psychosocial component to them. Bear in mind that the *manifestation* of disease is typically a lengthy process with many symptoms not showing up until adulthood, after years of unhealthiness. Again, I offer no simple answers as to why one becomes ill and another does not; in my opinion no person can do that. All I ask is that you take a moment to consider how our children's perspective of our world is shaped. Does it enhance the health of their soul, as well as their mind and body, or does it not?

Chapter Three

The Emergence of Pathophysiology from Energy Dysfunction

"You must be the change you wish to see in the world."

Mahatma Gandhi

Ever since I can remember, I longed for an affectionate and loving relationship with my mother, so much so I can actually relive the ache in my heart as a child. But my mother, the product of a broken home herself and the child of an unaffectionate and guarded mother, ultimately maintained emotional distance from her own children. Plus, my mother had more important things to do like work to put food on the table and a roof over mine and my sister's heads when she and my adulterous father divorced shortly after I was born. Along with those memories are the frequent times when I became ill with asthma, so ill it would demand my mother's undivided attention.

Then there came a time when I was about seven years old when my mother agreed to help a man care for his six year old daughter named "Linda" because his wife recently passed away. Linda was in our home, it seemed, all the time due to her father working long hours. I watched with dread as this stranger tried to move in on the already limited affections of my mother. Then she went so far as to call her "Mommy". Figuratively I felt my chest twisting with emotional pain. Realistically I had the worst asthma attack I had ever had, landing me in the hospital to receive large doses of epinephrine to open up my airway passages. Within days of returning home from the hospital I overheard my mother tell the girl's father that she could no longer help care for his daughter. When the man asked why, she replied that my physician suspected a strong emotional component to the triggering of my asthma attacks, and that she should explore what might be upsetting me. Noticing my behavior change when Linda entered our lives she logically made the connection.

Could my heartache and the false impressions of being unloved by my mother be associated with the onset of my asthma? Is it a coincidence that where I felt negative emotion is the same region where pathology emerged? Is it possible that because I was a "sensitive" child that I actually resonated with the subtle vibratory dynamics of my mother's own heartache from her failed marriage? What significance, if any, could disease possibly have outside of misfortune? Or might there be a message in relation to its development?

Traditional medicine certainly acknowledges a mind-body connection. However, the general consensus is that pathological changes first occur within the body *before* the mind can trigger and/or exacerbate symptoms of that disease. In other words in my case, emotional upset triggered asthma attacks within my already damaged lungs, not the other way around. And in some cases this is true. But traditional medicine is missing one important factor. And thankfully there is a small but growing group of health professionals that may finally be realizing that.

The well-being of an individual encompasses yet more than just the mind and body. There is a whole other determinant involved, and that is the health of the soul. One's mind cannot produce mentality without the soul; one's body cannot sustain life without the soul. The three, mind, body, and soul are intertwined, each influencing the other, naturally seeking balance. Therefore one cannot have true health without sound mind, body, *and* soul. Again, I present this chapter as food for thought. To know the absolute reason for another individual's afflictions would be to have access to their shared covenant with God, something I believe no human has. This chapter is intended for you to view health and the development of disease in a truly holistic manner, taking into account the precious balance of mind, body, and spirit, for our children and for ourselves.

WHAT MAKES KIDS SO DIFFERENT...

It goes without saying how we as adults have the responsibility of taking care of our children. We feed, clothe, protect, and of course, provide unconditional love for them. However, many of us are missing something when it comes to raising our children. We are overlooking their soul, perhaps because many of us sadly ignore our own.

And most important, how the souls of children differ from adults. They are unique in that they are very perceptive to spiritual energies; they are exceptionally and naturally intuitive. The souls of babies especially, being newly incarnated with limited means of communication, receive their information about other beings by means of perceiving their spiritual energy. As a child gets older, becomes accustomed to his physical environment, and forms his own rational opinion of the world and how to function within it, he slowly loses some of that sensitivity, some more so than others. And that is okay, as gradually the body makes use of the human senses to receive information in addition to what the soul perceives. However, we must take care of our children in a way that prevents the loss of receptivity to all spiritual impressions, because it is that

35

sensitivity which is essential to the preservation of our innate ability to intuit.

We as adults nurturing a new generation waste no time in teaching our young children the ABCs and 123s, then later we steer them toward what our worldly judgment says is success. But yet we tend to overlook the most spiritually fundamental of issues, the ones that measure success not by what we receive in life, but what we contribute. Our children need to understand that true happiness is never outside of ourselves and that a successful life results in wealth of the spirit, regardless of material gains. For even the most physically challenged child can not only live a spiritually fulfilled life, but can also promote the progression of all those he touches. In addition to all their other needs, it is to our children's benefit as they grow, that we ensure the wellness of the spirit. This statement will become clearer as you read on. What happens outside that precious nurturance is left to the direction of their own soul and God.

In the last chapter, I referred to two possible influences in the development of disease which I view as important in relation to raising our children: energy imbalance arising from spiritually repressive attitudes, beliefs and behaviors; and/or the "assimilation" or "taking in" of unhealthy subtle vibrational patterns of those who we share close, long-term relationships with. Allow me to assign terms to differentiate the two. The former I will call energy dysfunction stemming from *efferent imbalance* of the spirit, and the latter I will term *afferent imbalance*; adopted from the medical terms efferent, meaning "directing or bringing out from the body" and afferent, meaning "to bring toward the body". My intention is to gently ease you out of the conventional medicine mindset of viewing the body as a bio-machine, but   rather being a divine unification of mind, body, and soul; one that inherently seeks balance in order to truly be healthy.

EFFERENT IMBALANCE OF THE SPIRIT

Picture this. Seven year old boy on a soccer field playing his little heart out, squealing and genuinely having fun with the sport. Father on the sideline barking orders on how to play the game. Little boy approaches father during half-time only to hear him criticize him for not being an aggressive player, that playing the sport was all about winning, not about laughing and goofing off on the field. After the game during the ride home the father continues to criticize his son's soccer skills, and the boy begins to cry in the back seat of the car. Infuriated, the father calls the little boy a sissy and tells him only little girls cry. The boy holds back his tears and makes a silent vow to try harder in making his father proud of him.

Same little boy, pleased with himself, presents his parents with his second grade report card which shows him having a "B" average in academic subjects and an "E" for excellent conduct. Mother tells him she is disappointed that he did not get an "A" average and totally disregards the teacher's comment on her son's wonderful behavior in class. Little boy quickly concludes that it must be more important to achieve perfect grades than it is to treat others with respect and kindness. He vows to remember that in the future.

And day after day the little boy would listen to his father belittle just about everything his mother did, from making breakfast to what she wore for bed. He trusted nothing except the emotional numbing his hidden bottle of vodka gave him. His mother on the other hand was a chronic worrier, and the boy would watch as each day she would become overly anxious about the most trivial of things, like whether it as going to rain on the day when she shopped for food, or whether her desk would be dusted the way she liked it by the cleaning service at work. Overall the boy is raised in a very rigid manner, learning at an early age not to yield to the spontaneous nature of life itself; believing more and more that he is the sole owner and master of his existence. And as he grows he discovers quite effectively how to repress and protect his kind heart and sensitive spirit.

Fast forward thirty years. Now a man of thirty-seven years old he is the fiercely competitive owner of a successful computer manufacturing company. He has never married and has only been able to maintain relationships for brief periods at a time; probably because he cannot find someone as "perfect" as he is, and makes sure the woman he is with knows it. He is an aggressive, hostile, and over-controlling man. With an over-developed sense of urgency, he thinks nothing of impatiently pushing himself and his employees unmercifully toward what he perceives as excellence. Those who work for him dread his presence, and because he is so mistrusting of others he considers no one a "true" friend. His sense of identity is now formed by his success in business and his self-worth is measured by the amount of money he earns.

Health-wise, our young man suffers from frequent stomach ailments such as acid reflux. He is often seen around the office popping antacids in his mouth. Neither he, nor anyone else for that matter, would have ever guessed that his recent chest pains were in fact angina and not just heartburn. At age 38 he suffers a near-fatal heart attack, caused in part by years of undetected hypertension. The permanent damage of his young heart is a powerful wake-up call. Not only is he forced to abandon his pressured lifestyle, but his traumatic experience offers him a new perspective on life. Confrontation with death allows him to contemplate what it means to truly live. And what he now realizes is that the attitudes, beliefs, and behaviors he learned as a child, which effectively shielded his compassionate and delicate spirit, now became a suffocating suit of armor. Not only did it starve his heart of a vital sustenance called love but it also smothered the authentic radiance of his soul. It takes him years, but the young man finally rediscovers his soul and learns to live a life that serves its spiritual fulfillment.

What I just described to you was a possible example of someone who develops type A personality, an individual characterized as hostile, impatient, inappropriately competitive, and having time urgency. The science of medicine tells us that those who have type A personality are part of a variety of people who possess a set of responses to life events that are considered "maladaptive". Maladaptive responses are described as harmful physiological reactions to what an individual perceives as recurrent stress within their lives. According to study, maladaptive responses threaten the achievement of essential goals in life, specifically physical health, psychological health, and social functioning. A general model of illness states this occurs through prolonged disturbance of the delicate equilibrium of the body and its systems, ultimately affecting you both physically and mentally. Maladaptive responses can be so injurious that illnesses ranging from mental depression to even cancer have been suggested.

Sounds like medical mumbo jumbo for spiritual energy imbalance and subsequent physical dysfunction to me. And yes, while type A personality is a dramatic case in point, one need not have such extreme characteristics to suffer physical consequences. Any set of behaviors, attitudes, and beliefs which hinder a being's evolutionary growth can lead to the development of pathophysiology. Maladaptation, in a spiritual sense, can be seen as the deterrence or reluctance to live in a manner which serves the development of the soul. *This is what causes efferent energy imbalance;* the difficulty of living and seeing life as a sacred journey, one that purposely puts occurrences along your path for the modification of your soul. Spiritual imbalance in this case originates from energy distortions created by the secular mind. The series of events go like this: the mind, with its inhibiting perspective, initiates imbalance of the spirit, which then causes physiologic changes in the body. These physiologic changes, over time render you vulnerable to the development of illness and disease.

But efferent energy imbalance effects our lives in even more ways. Because our primary goal of incarnating is to realize spiritual truths, efferent imbalances alter our paths toward our desired life fulfillment. How? By continually placing opportunities for growth within that individual's path. Only those opportunities may become increasingly unpleasant until the spiritual truth is realized, if ever, in a lifetime. People who find themselves experiencing similar hardships within their lives over and over again are usually those who have yet to understand the "message in the misfortune". We must always try to look at obstacles as opportunities, a chance for betterment for ourselves and consequently for all those we share this space in time with. Interestingly, we realize that the medical term "maladaptive" has a further-reaching significance with regard to maturation of mind, body, and *soul*.

When we look at the development of disease via efferent energy imbalances we have a whole new insight as to how we may become unhealthy. Inherited diseases may not necessarily emerge from faulty genetic codes in the body, but rather from "faulty" beliefs and attitudes passed down from generation to generation. Examples of this are prejudice, hate, helplessness, and blame. With this thought in mind, is it possible then that certain illnesses might arise within a culture, race, or socioeconomic group from certain continuing group characteristics rather than inheritance? Challenge your current thinking and you will see how this is not only possible, but very true in certain cases. Indeed, various groups of man have progressed very much in terms of its civilization, however, many have yet to realize the more basic spiritual goals such as having a compassionate heart. Perhaps this is why heart disease is a leading cause of death in this society.

Let us take a closer look at how our little boy grew up. At an early age he learns that aggression is an effective way of getting what you want, whether it be physical or verbal aggression. After all, wasn't that the manner in which he was treated by the one of the most important people in his life? (Third chakra issue, [solar plexus], which may have initiated hypertension through constant stimulation of adrenal glands, and produce excessive gastric acid resulting in stomach ailments.) He also learns quickly that only perfection (or rather the illusion of), is worthy of recognition, even if achieving it is at the expense of others. (Again, third chakra issue. In addition, second chakra issues [sacral], result in problematic one on one relationships later in life.) Our little boy grows to see fault in everyone and everything, believing that if he could only control all things in his environment life would not be such a miserable disappointment. (Yet more energy distortion of the third chakra.) But perhaps the most detrimental belief our little boy holds is that he cannot genuinely and safely be his true self. His authentically loving, kind, and sensitive essence must be overcome by an integrally opposing persona. (Catastrophic energy distortion of the fourth chakra, the heart; starving it of not only the vital energy of love, but also of oxygen carrying blood.) In summary our little boy learned, through the most influential people in his life, how not to be himself. He also learned what spiritually repressive behaviors, attitudes, and beliefs to take on because they were ever-present in his family environment, and sometimes even rewarded.

How can we, as parents, relatives, teachers, and any other important figure in a child's life, ensure that they live life in accordance with their divine path and purpose? How can we do all we possibly can to assist them to reach their glorious potential, thus experiencing much needed spiritual progression for us all at this point of human evolution? First, we can start with ourselves. Efferent energy imbalances develop from how one views their existence, and we as adults need to take responsibility of how we influence our children's perception of their world. Are they left crying in their cribs at six months old because we are "training" them to sleep? Consider this, will we end up with a baby who can comfort themselves to sleep, or one that learns that because his cries for comfort and affection are ignored his needs are worthless? Are you repeating with your children some regretful things that your parents did to you? If so, you are not recognizing a divine opportunity for betterment. Yet, as you may notice, life will have a way of presenting those opportunities under different circumstances until we do realize it. We need to do some soul searching and take inventory of the ways in which we allow the repression our own souls and those we care for. My next several chapters can help you do that by offering you insight as to the true purpose of new life.

And while we may do the very best that we can, we must also understand that *misfortune may be part of an individual's path, an issue brought upon in the physical world from the spiritual for the purpose of working it out.* This is very different from the self-created efferent energy dynamics; it is part of a sacred plan between the entity (child or not) and our creator. As such there may be very little, if anything, that could alter that individual's course of life events. However, as always, unconditional love and prayer are powerful energies *always* felt by the soul, whether they improve worldly outcomes or not.

AFFERENT IMBALANCE OF THE SPIRIT

Imagine for a moment that a depressed friend of yours drops by for a visit. She barely says a word yet you *feel* emotionally, maybe even physically drained during, and perhaps for hours after her visit. That is temporary afferent imbalance; a spiritual energy dynamic which briefly changed

42

your flow of energy. It occurred because of a precious ability to share someone else's feelings so deeply that you had the capacity to experience her "same wavelength".

With children, especially babies, afferent energy imbalances can be manifested as sudden behavior change *of which there is not logical cause.* An example may be how when your very uptight mother-in-law stops by to visit, your perfectly content two month old angel suddenly breaks out in screams for no reason. She is not hungry, not wet, not in physical pain as far as you could tell. Yet when you hold her close she quiets easily. Mother-in-law gets her feelings hurt and you cannot figure out what just happened. The fact is baby's body was not in a state of discomfort, her soul was.

Be observant of a young child's behavior when they are in the company of another. Behaviors such as sudden withdrawal, clinginess, nervousness, or crying, again without obvious cause, may be indicative of an "uncomfortable" soul. The best remedy for this spiritual discomfort for the child is physical closeness to their parent or other trusted individual. It provides a sort of haven where the spiritual dynamics of the adult help in organizing the inner being of the child. More on this in chapter eleven.

I have a friend who was recently interviewing for a live-in nanny. She and her husband had four children ages 9, 4, 2, and 1. They met with about six women each on different occasions in their home with their young children present. Immediately they were grateful they had chosen to include their children in the interviewing process. All four had similar behavioral responses to each woman as they were being interviewed. Several women provoked immediate withdrawal from the children, others downright fear. Then came a woman who, without engaging the children at all, had all four warmly approach her. And by the end of the interview the 2 year old was actually upset that she was leaving. They, of course, chose this woman and so far are extremely pleased, not just because she is a good nanny, but more so because their children adore her.

The spiritual essences of most babies and some older children are not organized and stable, and therefore may be easily affected by the subtle energies of others. As I just described, the particular dynamics of a person's soul may have the power to rouse a tranquil baby, soothe an upset infant, and make a content child uneasy. Why can their essences be so unsound? Because it takes time for the soul to fully adapt and feel one with its new "body". It must get accustomed to the tremendous onslaught of new, and sometimes unpleasant sensations. Pain, temperature, hunger, and thirst, are just some of the startling sensations that the newly incarnated soul must deal with. That, along with having a limited means of communication is enough to make anyone desperate, insecure, and downright unraveled. In other words, what arrives to our world is an unorganized and terribly vulnerable little being.

However, I want to make it clear that afferent imbalance of the spirit does serve a purpose. It is the natural consequence of using intuition and should be carefully nurtured within our children. It serves a universal function in that it is meant to promote compassion through resonance with one another. This shared resonance is the thread of unity which connects us all as God's creations. Undoubtedly beneficial for evolution of the spirit, *as long as one has a stable and organized spiritual dynamic, and is resilient to extraneous energies.*

So how does one achieve this spiritual stability and resiliency for themselves as well as their children? First off, we must be a "spiritual" shelter for our children until their souls become organized and secure, which usually occurs by the time they reach nine years of age. Allow your child to cling to you when he is unsure or uncomfortable in his surroundings. It is his way of trying to organize, restore and/or "recharge" his inner being and thus will gain a feeling of wholeness and security.

Next, strive for the most fundamental balance of them all, the absolute integration of mind, body, and soul. In other words, in order to assist our children in becoming resilient individuals, yet still be receptive to the spiritual impressions which form intuition, we must help our children to realize and live in harmony with their soul. No small task indeed, but read on and I will help you by taking you on their journey to our world. Because when you realize the true purpose of new life, the spirit in all is revealed.

Efferent Imbalance of the Spirit: "Energy directing or bringing out from the body"	Afferent Imbalance of the Spirit: "Energy brought toward the body"
Causes: Spiritual imbalance in this case originates from energy distortions created by the secular mind. The series of events go like this: the mind, with its inhibiting perspective, initiates imbalance of the spirit, which then causes physiologic changes in the body. These physiologic changes, over time render you vulnerable to the development of illness and disease.	**Causes:** Temporary afferent imbalance is a spiritual energy dynamic which briefly changes the flow of the energy in and around the body. It occurs because of a precious ability to share someone else's feelings so deeply that you have the capacity to experience the "same wavelength".
Implications for our children: Because the development of disease is most often a lengthy process, taking years to manifest its symptoms, a healthy foundation begins in childhood with the well being of a child's soul. Efferent energy imbalances develop from how one views their existence and we as adults need to take responsibility of how we influence our children's perception of their world.	**Implications for our children:** The spiritual essences of most babies and some older children are not organized and stable and therefore may be easily affected by the subtle energies of others. The particular dynamics of a person's soul may have the power to rouse a tranquil baby, soothe an upset infant, and make a content child uneasy. It takes time for the soul to fully adapt and feel one with its new "body". It must get accustomed to the tremendous onslaught of new, and sometimes unpleasant sensations. In other words, what arrives to our world is an unorganized and terribly vulnerable little being who is very sensitive to extraneous energies.

THE DAWN OF ENLIGHTENMENT FOR MEDICINE

As I mentioned earlier, there is a growing number of health professionals who are changing their ideas about traditional medicine. This is largely because within the last decade or so research in the field of medicine is showing an undeniable mind-body-spirit connection when it comes to overall health, life fulfillment, and general sense of well-being. Such elusive practices as spiritual energy work (Reiki, Therapeutic Touch, acupuncture, etc.), meditation, and prayer have all been shown to facilitate health by enhancing the body's recovery, increasing pain control, and improving the ability to cope with mental and physical trauma. Spirituality has been discovered as the foundation of this optimized health. What exactly is it about spirituality that offers miraculous outcomes? It imparts purpose and meaning to all things in one's life; it allows the mortal self to let go of the illusion of having full control of one's path; it is the understanding that love is the nucleus of all existence. All of that (and then some), awakens the mind, body, and soul to a vibratory level consistent with what one defines as health. It promotes holistic balance.

So with the manifestation of symptoms of disease usually occurring after years of disharmony, would it not stand to reason that we should be routinely observing the well-being of our children's soul, as well as their mind and body? In what way are we not allowing the true expression of their spirit? In what way are we shaping their perspective of their world? What illusions in life are we perpetrating that say *we* have the ultimate control of our own outcomes? And the myth that true happiness is achieved by things acquired through worldly possessions. How are we failing in having them realize just how magnificent, deliberate, and courageous their arrival to our

47

world is?

It is now said that children who suffer from asthma wear their hearts on their sleeves. After all these years I suspect my own affliction with the disease may be a consequence of my "sensitivity". Sensing both the false message of being unloved by my only parent, and the possibility of perceiving my mother's own heartache and strife as a single mother. I believe it was no coincidence that where I felt strong negative emotion was the same region where physical dysfunction emerged.

And although emotional upset is a known potential trigger for an asthmatic event the vast majority of medical researchers believe that lung changes occurred long before the triggers are identified. But what I want you to think about is how did those lung changes occur in the first place? Asthma is one of the many diseases for which researchers have found no basic cause; yet approximately 20 million Americans suffer from it each year. And of those diseases that a cause can be identified, what makes the afflicted region of the body so vulnerable? I suspect that as research continues to explore the impact of human holism on health, science will have no choice but to recognize and address the role of the spirit. And it will be then that the "experts" will routinely advise us on how to care for the integrity of our children's soul as part of their well-being. For those of you reading this book, that time has already come.

PART TWO

PRE-CONCEPTION: PLANNING FROM THE HEAVENS

CHAPTER FOUR

WHY WE VISIT "SCHOOL EARTH"

"In times of change, learners inherit the Earth, while the learned find themselves beautifully equipped to deal with a world that no longer exists."

Eric Hoffer

First and foremost, when speaking about "planning from the heavens" I must tell you that your soul and/or your partner's will *know* the soul of the child that is to be yours. Whether you both are already parents or about to become parents, whether the child is a biological product of you or not, your soul can and will recognize this timeless companion. How do you know when you encounter a spiritual companion? It feels like instant recognition of someone, as though you have known them forever, an unmistakable awakening of the heart that resounds within the depths of your soul. Sound familiar? Might you have experienced that same feeling with your significant other? A best friend? A niece, a nephew? I am sure you know what I am talking about. That curious recognition, that strange familiarity is basically the result of meeting a kindred spirit, a being who you share a timeless relationship with. That precious child (or children) in your life is undoubtedly a soul companion, one who you may share the

51

most powerful relationship during this lifetime with, in terms of achieving spiritual wisdom and progression. A relationship that can give both of your souls the opportunity to grow like no other.

Your child, just as all of us, will be born with the goal of achieving spiritual growth and development through the use of human experience. Lovingly encouraged by a Higher Power and assisted by her Guides, she carefully selects a situation which would best foster this development. Parents, siblings, race, sex, socioeconomic status, etc. are all part of a multidimensional process of choice which all souls undergo when returning to "school Earth". It is important to understand that as discarnate souls we are *involved* in the process of choosing our incarnate situation. It is a decision based on our evolutionary issues. Why is this so important for you to understand? For two reasons. First, it helps you to see through the illusions of randomness in life. And second, it discourages contempt and blaming God when "bad" things happen to "good" or "innocent" people, especially children. Yes, as difficult as it is to accept, there is healing, balancing, and even justice in events we see as tragic. This statement will become clearer as you read on.

The choices we make and consequences we live through during our incarnated existence mature us and allow us to spiritually progress. The situations we choose usually involve familiar entities within our particular soul group, sort of like members of a large family. Your spiritual family is that of peers, souls who share similarities with you in respect to spiritual evolution. In other words, it is very likely that you are moving through your spiritual development with the same group of entities lifetime after lifetime. Be assured, the children you have or are about to have, are with you for a reason greater than you may now comprehend. The experiences you have with your child can potentially provide the most intense learning that both she and you will have.

You see, as souls on our journey toward evolution we often form developmental pacts with those in our spiritual groups. Sibling one lifetime, lover next; enemy one lifetime, comrade another. Depending on the specific spiritual issues we need to address and mature from, our "soul peers" may lend a hand in our reaching those developmental goals. And very significant issues may be worked through with the help of a soul peer(s) who will encourage your spirit's growth. Among everyone else in our lives, a beloved child can evoke the most profound growth of all, and vice versa. The parent/child relationship can literally make or break the soul's quest toward attaining its evolutionary goals.

Just think back to your own upbringing. If you are like most of us you may not have had a picture perfect childhood. Many of us grew up in less than model situations. Perhaps you had an overly oppressive and protective mom, or maybe a neglectful one; a tyrannical dad, or possibly no dad at all. However your relationship was with your parent(s), whatever pain or happiness they brought you, you can be sure there was nothing coincidental about their presence, or absence, in your life. You, like your child, chose your situation to be born into; the choice is meant to carry out spiritual maturation.

An exceptionally kind and sympathetic friend of mine once confided in me that she had a truly miserable childhood. Having an alcoholic father and an abusive mother she often endured harsh beatings. She also saw things no child should ever witness. Like the many times her mother forced her teenage brother to drag their intoxicated and belligerent father home from the local bar. Like the numerous times her father physically assaulted her mother, and the time her teenage sister almost committed suicide. My dear friend told me that she felt so sorry for that little girl she once was. However, she now realizes how living through such tribulation made her the strong-willed yet caring person she is today. And how she has grown from her experience into a fierce advocate for children.

Progression through pain, spiritual growth is indeed the intended outcome of such circumstances.

Or, your child may encourage the growth of your soul. I am sure most people would agree with me that there is no greater pain than a parent losing a child. Yet, through human choice, such a devastating loss can initiate a series of events that end up bringing great benefit to many other people. Let me explain.

Say for example, my soul needs to learn and demonstrate compassion for another. It is one of the divine truths my essence must experience in order to progress at this point of my own evolution. Prior to our incarnation, you, as my soul peer, lovingly agree to help me with this task. You have consented to be my child, and during our worldly existence your physical body has succumbed to a rare congenital disorder. I, through the emotional pain of my loss, *choose* to re-direct that energy for others in a positive way. I am motivated to start bereavement groups to help all those who have similarly lost loved ones to any congenital disorder, thus helping thousands of people through heartfelt compassion.

These spiritual dynamics are the nature of our development. Grief, as with any pain, is a human experience, an experience not intended to be cruel but instead benevolent. The loss of a loved one, whether by physical death or separation, may be meant to bring about change, change which provokes your spirit to expand and progress. That you face such hardship is a covenant born of love between you and God. Working as a social worker and then a nurse I have seen a wide spectrum of human suffering. The most debilitating of all responses to hardship are helplessness and hopelessness; believing that God is somehow punishing you for something you have done, and therefore becoming powerless and/or indignant.

This is not to say though that your life is predestined. I believe you create a new destiny with every human choice you make. But specific objectives for growth are determined for a certain lifetime, and opportunities to meet those objectives continually arise until they are met. And indeed we are not alone in our journey. Our ever-present spiritual Guides and Teachers try to gently steer us in the right direction each time we encounter roadblocks in our learning endeavors. And if spiritual growth is not attained during this lifetime then we simply must address that development in a subsequent lifetime.

SIBLINGS, TWINS, AND OTHER MULTIPLES:
LIFETIME SOUL PARTNERS

Whether a child is a sibling to one or many, or whether he/she is part of a multiple gestation, one thing holds true. Brothers and sisters share a unique, and what may seem mysterious bond. I am sure you have heard the amazing true stories. Brother and sister who were separated as toddlers spend most of their adult lives trying to find each other. Though reared in opposite coasts they coincidently find each other while having dinner with a mutual friend. Teenage twin girls, one was unable to articulate words because of being born with cerebral palsy. Yet the sister routinely communicates with her disabled twin telepathically and does the talking for her. And of course let us not leave out those well documented cases of twins reared apart who share strikingly similar attributes such as specific talents, tastes in clothing and hairstyle, and choice of vocation. Separated by distance these siblings are found to practically be living parallel lives.

So what is it that mysteriously ties siblings to one another? Much more than sharing a genetic relationship, they are beings who possess a spiritual bond. Having similar evolutionary issues souls who choose to incarnate into a brotherhood do so with expectations of transcendent reciprocity. In other words, born as siblings they have agreed to work together toward spiritual progression. And whether by way of camaraderie or by animosity, siblings possess a unique give and take existence within the physical world which undoubtedly is meant to serve the development of their souls. What's more, within a group of soul peers one who incarnates as a sibling would likely be one who has shared numerous lifetimes with the other. And as such, they have become mutual partners, oftentimes having similar "innate" qualities, not because of similar genes, but because of having a timeless kinship.

Let us consider an extreme example of lifetime soul partners, conjoined twins. What benefit could possibly emerge from such a seemingly cruel arrangement of physical bodies? Plenty. Two souls living their physical existence as a conjoined body experience the most fundamental of spiritual morals in a very profound way. Just think about it. Their lives subsist on cohesion, patience, empathy, selflessness, and harmonization. Depending on where they are conjoined these siblings *intuitively* coordinate the voluntary actions of their blended bodies, showing us all the expression and connectedness of the soul. If not surgically separated you will likely hear them loudly oppose the very thought of disjoining. Embodying the very nature of what we are now still trying to learn globally: That we are all one and the same. And that perhaps if we can learn their virtues, we too can learn to live in harmony. I believe conjoined twins are not only deeply bound to their own spiritual development, but that they also symbolize something far greater to our human race in general.

Wake Up, Time for School!

The birth of every baby holds a new opportunity for spiritual evolution, not only for herself, but for all creation

56

whom she shares that time with. Like the tiniest pebble dropping into the center of a pond, every part of the water is touched by the wake it creates. And no matter how brief or how long her stay, human existence will never again be the same as before her arrival. The goal always being progression of the soul.

The analogy of school is often used to help one understand the concept our soul's intention to "learn" or realize divine truths while incarnated. In using this analogy, we are all "students" in a system of education. During elementary school you and your fellow classmates progress through the grades together; sometimes helping each other, other times engaging in a few school yard fights. One grade school year (lifetime) you may have an antagonistic relationship with someone, only to fall madly in love with them later in high school (different lifetime). And during summer vacation (between lifetimes) you and your guidance counselor (celestial Guides/Teachers) reflect upon your scholastic accomplishments. Together you discuss and plan your goals for when you return to school in the Fall (subsequent lifetime). Either you progress to the next grade (evolve spiritually), or repeat the last if learning was not achieved (address same unattained spiritual goals during subsequent lifetime).Consequently, the elements involved in the spirit's planning of its incarnation are so numerous, multifaceted, and interwoven it would be impossible for me to present them all. Aside from developmental goals, family, race, sex, socioeconomic status, and so much more is considered with regard to what situation a soul is born into.

Of significant relevance to the choices is the period of time, within the existence of earth, when one would elect to be incarnated. What I am about to describe may be somewhat difficult for one to conceptualize because of its abstract nature. I ask that you take with you what rings true in your own essence, whatever does not, just skip through in these next paragraphs.

Time, as we know it, is linear; always moving forward, forever predictable. One o'clock will precede two o'clock, Monday will precede Tuesday, 1990 is a decade later than 1980. However, what if I were to tell you that time is simply an illusion, existing only in the physical world to provide structure within the framework of our chosen life experience. That depending on our own spiritual evolution and needs we choose a time in space that would best suit our development. The time in space in which we choose to live in is, as I mentioned before, is shared with those entities in our peer group whom will support our growth. Stay with me here.

As children in school we are taught to plot Earth's history on a timeline. I remember drawing timelines to demonstrate the development of early man, from Cro-Magnon to Neanderthal. A two-dimensional image of time, inherently having a beginning and an end. Now try to visualize yourself in the center of a three-dimensional sphere observing "time" float around you horizontally in a circle. The end blends with the beginning, and the beginning blends with the end, absolutely seamless. All of "time" surrounds you and as you take a closer look you can see how certain eras in time serve certain needs of spiritual development. Each era, like video film, is made up of individual frames running vertically. Within each frame exists a reality based on personal choice and the consequences of that choice on all creation at that moment in time. In other words, the era you chose to live in indeed has a history but there exists, in separate frames, many other histories as well, made up of the consequences of different human choices. Furthermore, along that same circle of "time" also exists what we would consider to be the future; frames of reality not accessible to the incarnated soul as history by means of physical evidence, (i.e. historic recording, fossils, etc.). Therefore past lives may not occur in the past at all, but simply as a reality that best serves a soul's stage of evolution.

To some, what I just said will make perfect sense. Nevertheless, what is important to understand is that we are all energetically connected to one another. Right now, as incarnated souls we are all sharing the same "frame of film", so to speak. United, we determine the pace of our spiritual advancement and our soul's search for wisdom. Will we in fact progress as a group, or regress? A human choice with spiritual consequence.

You will hear many people who have undergone a Near Death Experience describe a scenario where they witness their lives played out in front of them like they are viewing a movie. However, the scenes they witness are of specific times in their lives when they have had to make choices. Choices which they then realized as discarnate beings, greatly impacted their journey toward evolution. Simultaneously, these people report observing the consequences of their choices on others whom they have shared their incarnated existence with. Alternatives to those choices may also be shown as well as the reality reflecting those different choices.

So what, you may ask, does all this have to with a child's journey into being? Everything. Before conception even occurs there is the soul, and that soul has a history, a present, and a future. It has an agenda for his/her life, and although intermingled with the lives of its chosen family its soul is not a reflection of those it physically resembles. He may have the same color eyes as his mother, the same feet as his father, and the same wavy hair as his brother, but know that a child's soul is purely unique. Conception is just part of the continuum of a soul's existence, the journey into emerging greatness. The role of the parents and all those of authority around the child is to honor the process by protecting, nurturing, and facilitating the blossoming of the spirit.

I will be discussing in the next chapters the three main catalysts that nudge a soul to return to body. These motives are not exclusive of one another and may in fact overlap, depending on the developmental goals of all involved. You will hear me say this many times, though simple, it is a key concept in this book. We are all born with a purpose, whether it is for self-development or to selflessly aid in the development of another individual or group. Even the baby who takes only a couple of breaths outside the womb before its demise has a purpose. Perhaps for reasons not available to us in body there is learning and healing in death itself.

CHAPTER FIVE

SELF-DEVELOPMENT OF THE SOUL

"A master can tell you what he expects of you. A teacher, though awakens your own expectations."

Patricia Neal

Imagine for a moment the unborn child contemplating the needs of his own soul. He is "home" sitting among a spectacular meadow immersed in absolute beauty. Along side of him is his Guide, a powerful entity who serves as a beloved mentor. Together they reflect on the maturation and wisdom the unborn child has achieved so far, along with any shortcomings. Choices and actions from all prior embodied experiences are reviewed. There may be an upcoming opportunity to share a time and space with some of his soul peers, and join them in a mutual quest for continued growth during that era of existence. However, the unborn entity is suddenly aware of all the harshness that comes with acquiring a physical body. The sensations of pain, hunger, and thirst alone, are enough reason for him to be reluctant to be born. Yet when he does some more self-examination he knows he must take this opportunity despite his hesitance. His Guide lovingly assures him that he, as well as other Higher Beings, will be with him every step of his physical existence. His inner being need only be open to their guidance.

Quite an imaginative scene I agree, but it does not stray far from the celestial accounts of persons who have experienced Near-Death episodes. Some of these individuals claim that during the time of their death they meet with a Higher Being and subsequently review the choices and consequences of very momentous times in their lives. These scenes are played before them in an instantaneous manner. And in what seems like a fraction of a second they become immensely aware of any wrong directions taken in their lives. Suddenly, what their purpose is, what path they were meant to follow becomes crystal clear. When resuscitated they awaken with an altered view of their life and will oftentimes change it to achieve greater fulfillment. Fulfillment, that is, of the endeavors of the spirit, not the physical being. A moment of consultation with their Angel was all that was needed to realign their lives with what they agreed to, *before* they were born.

So what are the issues that behold the power of spiritual growth? What exactly are we talking about achieving with the guidance of our Higher Beings? Essentially, what are some of the multifaceted reasons for the physical birth of each and every child? And yes, I did say reason. For even the "surprise" arrival of a child has unequivocal purpose for its coming.

What I am about to discuss is just one aspect of the true meaning of new life. The information is derived from years of studying health and wellness through the eyes of psychology, sociology, medicine, and finally numerous cultural contributions. One resounding truth I have discovered and share with many is that wellness is far beyond the removal of symptoms, and true contentment is not attained through materialistic gains. It is in part the harmonization of mind, body, and spirit; it is also the realization of power and knowledge far beyond the limits of physicality. It is what imparts inner peace, what instills the sense of completion at our hour of physical death. This chapter directs you back to the dynamics of the chakras and layers of the spiritual energy field, for within them lies the reflection of each individual's journey toward greatness.

Recall in Chapter 2 how spiritually repressive attitudes, beliefs, and behaviors can lead to the bodily imbalance responsible for the development of disease. This happens when the delicate equilibrium generated by our chakras gets disturbed as a result of secular issues. What often determines the health of the chakras is in part the degree by which we live our lives according to the spiritual truths represented within these energy centers of the human body. The following is a look at the spiritual truths each chakra represents and mirrors within the body. I offer it as a means of helping you understand one aspect of the true purpose of new life. By all means it is not the only reason why a child arrives to our world. The next chapter discusses several other forces which motivate an entity toward physical birth.

Chakra 1 - Root: Located at the base of the spine this chakra takes in vital life energy from the earth and all of nature around us. The spiritual truth inherent in the root chakra is that we are all born with purpose. Our journey into being is as deliberate as the creation of all else we share this world with. We are connected to nature and all of creation around us. And what affects one, affects us all. A fully functional root chakra promotes a feeling of being grounded and belonging to our world. It is evidenced by a person who has a powerful presence and vitality (you *feel* it when this person walks into a room). They enjoy being alive and handle life's challenges well. Trials and tribulations are viewed as opportunities for strength to emerge as they are meant to awaken the soul to needed change.

The root chakra also reflects our issues of survival and how well we manage our physical existence. It mirrors our trust and security in our means of sustenance, our possessions, and of life itself. It reveals the comfort of simply being in our physical world.

Empowering our children through truth: Logically we must communicate to our children from the moment they are born (perhaps even before their birth), that their arrival is filled with universal intent. We must convey that the world welcomes their courageous journey. And we should do what we can to instill a sense of safety and security in their existence. Teach them that regardless of any challenges they face they should never feel threatened nor fearful to live their lives to the fullest.

To further guide our children we could promote their awareness of how we share our world with all of creation. Show them how the earth too requires balance by having all of its inhabitants live in coherence. And how respecting God's creations allows a reciprocal exchange of vibrational reverence that will last eternally. The earth too has an essence and together we make up its aura.

Chakra 2 - Sacral: Located just below our navel this chakra is involved with issues of creativity, procreation, emotions, and one on one relationships. Where the first chakra dealt with our relationship with all things in nature, our second chakra deals with interpersonal bonds. This can mean any person to person connection, like we share with our lovers, family members, friends, and colleagues. The well known proverb "Do unto others as you would have done unto you", would appropriately capture the message of this chakra. It reveals how we treat the people in our lives.

Furthermore, this energy center directs that the soul be capable of establishing close relationships with one another. This includes feeling safe with intimacy and communion. The ability to honor close relationships, and not abuse the power of having the affections of someone else is basic. Using control in this manner may adversely affect the vibrational stability of the chakra that mirrors our bonds with others.

Another aspect of our sacral chakra reveals our need as humans to produce, to express ourselves through the power of creativity. This can mean any form of creation, from something as minor as drawing a picture to something as grand as conceiving a child.

Empowering our children through truth: We can demonstrate this truth from the moment our children are born. The first relationship your baby is aware of after birth is the bond with his primary caregiver, usually his mother. As a primary caretaker we must be conscientious about swiftly responding to our infant's needs, for this becomes the basis of trust for our children's relationships to come. Furthermore, if we treat others in our family unit with care, honor, and respect it easily becomes the foundation of how our children learn to treat others. Acquiring mistrust, dishonor, and immorality as a child may render him incapable of establishing close, life promoting bonds with others as he matures in adulthood.

Our child should be allowed emotional and creative expression within a safe and loving environment. And once our child is old enough she should be taught that sex is a healthy aspect of life. An expression of our spiritual desire to commune with another human being that ought to be upheld with some reverence.

Chakra 3 - Solar Plexus: Located just above the naval and below the sternum the solar plexus relates to all things about ourselves; the energy of our self-esteem, self-worth, and self-image are all contained in this chakra. Herein lie issues of personal power, ego, and identity. Also, the perception of awakening intuition is felt here, hence the commonly known saying "gut feeling".

So much can be said about the soul's third chakra. But perhaps the most intriguing fact regarding new life is that this is the region of the body where the vital energy of the spirit integrates with the physical body just before birth, through infancy, and sometimes lasting beyond preschool. Attached to the etheric layer in the womb via an "umbilical cord" of spiritual energy, the third chakra is where the physical body meets the spiritual body at the moment of birth, (see illustration). How the integration of body and soul proceed from birth is determined by both the naked character of the incoming spirit and the kind of nurturing the newborn child receives. (More on this subject in the next part of this book.) As such, the manner in which we nurture our children can have a profound effect on the "health" of their third chakra, greatly shaping their sense of selves and personal power. Consequently, the solar plexus is the chakra affected most when a child is abused or neglected. Events of maltreatment are "recorded" in this energy center creating imbalances that may endure well into adulthood leading to dysfunction of the stomach, liver, pancreas, gallbladder, and kidneys. Emotionally, the child may grow to have chronic anxiety, fear, and hindering insecurities. This is the individual, young or old, who takes *in* the energy of others. She is also the one likely to have problems with addictions.

Conversely, the solar plexus can also become dysfunctional when a growing child is infantilized and not given the opportunity to mature and take responsibility for herself. Both circumstances can bestow a sense of powerlessness, rendering a child inadequate in asserting her own will.

We as adults must be mindful that *the energy dynamics of infants and children can be adversely affected by events despite their ability to mentally recollect the experience.* Therefore, an infant *can* be affected by persistent disregard of his cries for comfort. The inner being of a two year old child *can* be scarred when treated with hostility or indifference. And as I just mentioned, these dysfunctional patterns of a child's spiritual energy may continue their destructive path up to and throughout adulthood, giving rise to both the physical and psychological problems described above.

Empowering our children through truth: Telling our children that they are unique, worthy, talented, and beautiful creations of a loving God can start as early as conception. One of the greatest gifts we can give them is assistance in realizing their true magnificent selves, help them to exist without insecurities and to discover their powerful "naked" inner selves.

I ask that for a moment you think about how difficult that can be for our children these days. We currently live in a society that places so much emphasis on physical beauty and external power that it becomes easy to lose sight of the magnificence of our inner being. An arsenal of media bombards our children each day with images of what men and women should look like and what defines ultimate success. Children younger and younger are idolizing people simply on the basis of their celebrity or earning power. Actors, musicians, models, and millionaires are being worshiped regardless of the content of their character. Some of whom are not even comfortable in their *own* skins let alone be an icon for imitation. How easy is it for our children to be seduced into wanting the same things that give these people extraordinary admiration, such as "perfect" looks, or the power to make a lot of money, even if it means doing something against their very nature. Eating disorders, anxiety and depressive disorders can easily develop as our children struggle to build self esteem on an image that does not reflect their authentic selves. Compounded with their loss of identity and sense of spiritual emptiness, the desire for our youth to medicate their pain by abusing substances such as alcohol and drugs becomes almost understandable.

The full integration of body and soul can be a lifelong quest for many, for it is the achievement of accessing a fulfillment not attained through worldly successes. As the parent of an infant the best we can do for her is to ease her transition from spirit to spirit and body. And we do this by frequently embracing her, skin to skin contact, carrying her in slings or other close contact carriers, and promptly attending to her needs. Essentially bathing her in the radiance of your own loving energies helps your baby to organize the chaos of *her* inner being. Quieting your baby's soul in this way conserves precious energy, energy needed to conform to the newness of her physical body.

As the child grows the fundamental goal relating to the solar plexus would be assisting her to discover her magnificent inner self, help her find the strengths of her soul, and challenge the weaknesses she brought forward. It is about her loving and living in harmony with her inner self. With that, personal power is accomplished, along with the confidence that her place in this world is filled with purpose regardless of the "skin" she was born into.

Chakra 4 - Heart: The heart chakra is located just where implied at the mid-sternum. Herein lie issues of love for self, love for others, forgiveness, hope, trust, and compassion. This is the energy center that reflects our capacity to receive love fully and to love ourselves completely. An open heart chakra reveals the ability to forgive, cleansing the soul of resentments, grudges, and hurts, not only toward others but towards ourselves. It is special in that its energy radiates through and influences the other charkas, giving it the capability of filling our being with healing vibratory sustenance. The "heart" of the soul is the part of us that recognizes our unity as creations of God, and therefore allows us to perceive the beauty in life itself. Indeed the power of the fourth chakra is palpable. Just think for a moment at a time when you felt intense love. Beginning in the chest your whole body warms, your arms and legs may tingle, your facial expression changes, and tears may fill your eyes. This is the energy of the heart chakra blooming, spreading its radiance throughout the workings of your soul. It is the same radiance which embraces the child in the arms of his loving parent, and it is the energy center stimulated when an infant suckles at the breast of his mother. This essence bathes the child providing serenity for his mind, body *and soul*.

Cardiovascular disease, diabetes, lung cancer, breast cancer, and immune-related disorders are among the various illnesses most prevalent in our society, and a few are steadily rising in numbers. And I, along with many others, believe their development is more complex than science maintains; involving an aspect of our existence that *includes* the emergence of typical risk factors. In other words, the tendency to smoke, become obese, or for our bodies to abnormally raise cholesterol levels may purely be part of the pathological energy flow within our own inner beings. The manifestation of disease is essentially the end result of energy dysfunction which triggered the very same risk factors such as overeating or becoming addicted to a substance.

Let me give you an example. My close friend's father has six siblings, most obese, some have diabetes, some smoke, others abuse substances. And all are now unfortunately at high risk for cardiovascular disease. My friend's father however, stands out from the rest of his family because he has never had any of these problems. Interestingly, when asked about his childhood the one thing he will tell you he remembers most is his mother being very critical and unaffectionate with her children, all of them except for him. He is the oldest of the seven and was always praised and given much more affection as a child from his mother than any of his siblings. In fact, as adults now, his brothers and sisters occasionally joke how he was always the "preferred" kid in the family.

Other possible influences notwithstanding, could their mother's emotional distance (affecting heart energy) and disapproving manner (affecting solar plexus energy) with her other children have anything to do with their problems of over-eating? Addictions? In these cases the *behaviors* triggered by emotional voids logically led to disease. Is it any surprise then that organs in the region of the heart and abdomen are the ones afflicted? Not when you realize where and how long the energy dysfunction loomed in those body regions in the first place. All of which began in childhood.

The development of disease is never an overnight process, you will hear me say this often. Subtle changes in our spiritual bodies caused by emotions or ways of thinking can lead not only to the impaired cellular function seen as precursors of disease, but also to the *behaviors* considered to be risk factors for disease. Once again our children's health involves addressing the totality of their existence, mind, body, and spirit.

Empowering our children through truth: There are four essential elements to impart on our precious little ones as they grow: 1) They are absolutely and unequivocally worthy of love without conditions. 2) That they are to love themselves entirely regardless of their weaknesses or shortcomings. 3) That they themselves must give love openly without expectations or conditions. 4) That they must allow themselves to forgive, not only others but themselves for any wrongdoings done throughout their lives.

Loving others with reservations is so easy. Just think about it. Would you continue to love your spouse if he or she was unfaithful to you? Would you continue to love your best friend if he or she betrayed your trust? The same goes for forgiveness. How long would you close your heart off to compassion for others and yourself because of old hurts, resentments or grudges? It is hard to let go and allow love to seep back into your heart, especially when we have been hurt really bad. It seems simpler to keep the invisible wall around the heart intact, that way it cannot be penetrated again.

But love and forgiveness go hand and hand as they are the fundamentals of an open heart. They are powerful elements that we must be mindful in ourselves as well as our children because not only do our children imitate behaviors, but also attitudes, ways of thinking, and matters of the heart. Even if you show *them* unconditional love they may still, for example, perceive your lack of self-love, or your tendency to hold onto anger for years. Thus setting the stage for the same type of imbalances I described earlier.

Those who understand the importance of spiritual well-being have known what I am writing all along. But now research has recently shown that indeed our physical health is adversely affected when we refuse forgiveness and when we lack compassionate human bonds. Both were linked to (again, no surprise here) cardiovascular disease and impaired immune function. Little by little science will someday get the "whole picture". At least I hope they do for the sake of future generations. With regard to guiding our children it may help to understand that forgiveness is not about forgoing injustice or reconciling with the people who hurt you or condoning their behavior. We should teach how instead it is an internal state of acceptance, a letting go of anger and suffering. We now have medical research that supports the claim that a life without loving relationships, compassionate human bonds, and heartfelt forgiveness can be detrimental to the health of an individual. Sounds like spiritual advice to me. Nonetheless, please pass it on, for yourself, for our children, for our future.

Chakra 5 - Throat: Located in the center of the neck this chakra involves issues of expression, communication, choice, self-discipline, and will. It is the thruway which bridges the heart and the mind. A powerful part of the soul because it has the ability to wound others and ourselves easily through vocal indiscretions.

Our inner being must have the capacity to express itself, to assert its will, and to vocally communicate the strength of its spirit. A fully functioning throat chakra enables the soul to orally purge itself of thoughts and emotions that affect its integrity. Even in the absence of formal language the soul can communicate through the energy of this chakra by means of crying, laughing, shouting, and other vocalizations. In fact one of the goals of psychotherapy is to "open" this energy center by encouraging verbal catharsis.

When the soul is in harmonious balance this center is used for positivism. Choosing vocalization with the intent to harm causes distortion of the energy in this chakra. As we are all creations of the same Higher Being we are not to use the power of this fifth energy center to communicate hate, prejudice, or contempt toward our fellow man.

Strength of personal will including wise discernment and decision making are also reflected in this chakra. Self-discipline is part of this energy center as well in that it requires the use of personal will. In other words, in order to make personal changes in our lives, say for example to exercise more, we need both the will and self-discipline to carry the task through; the two must be in agreement. And it requires a certain amount of introspection and soul searching to apply self-discipline, which is always a step toward reaching a state of higher awareness.

Empowering our children through truth: During infancy we listen and respond to our children's laughter, their cries, their cooing, and their screams whether from delight or fright. A baby will in fact use all kinds of vocalization as a way to express what is going on inside of her. And we as adults understand this because logically she does not yet know language. We realize these are some of the ways our baby communicates with us. All our baby expects us to do is *respond.* When we persistently fail to respond to their attempts of communicating we in effect encourage the silence of their soul. What may emerge is a child who is withdrawn and unconfident of the value and needs of her own inner being.

Many people used to believe that if you responded often to a young child when they were upset that you would end up "spoiling" him or her. In fact even now there are some from the older generations who may still believe in this fallacy. I cannot imagine how anyone could advise parents or other caregivers to refrain from comforting their own child when he or she cries out for them; it goes against the very nature of parenting and betrays all instincts. It saddens me that "experts" today can still advise parents to ignore a young child's cries for the purpose of training them to sleep. Not only does this diminish any intuitive bonding that occurs between parent and child but it also poses a risk for baby. The parent or caregiver who persistently ignores a child's cry increases their likelihood of not picking up on signs of impending illness or even danger. To validate the worth of our inner beings no one should be ignored, much less a young child.

As a child grows older she will normally add the use of language to express herself. Resist the temptation to silence our children as so many of us do when we are stressed ourselves. If you miss the chance to listen, return later with the intent of giving her your undivided attention. Vocalization is a powerful means of expression for the soul. Listening to our children as they play, laugh, argue, and cry not only shows that they are valued but also provides an opportunity to gaze into the strengths and weaknesses of their inner being. And *perceiving* the soul of your child is the key to intuitive nurturing. A great advantage in gently guiding our children to their adult years.

Chakra 6 - Brow: Whirling above the brow in the center of the forehead is the chakra also known as the "third eye". This energy center contains issues of clarity, insight, and mental processes including the capacity to learn. Herein also lies the ability to visualize through the eyes of the soul. Clairvoyance and the ability to accurately perceive the energies of the spiritual world are possible when this chakra is open and free of dysfunctional energy flow.

The inherent lesson of the brow chakra is to see truth. It reflects the soul's capacity for honest and accurate insight into itself and the world around us. It is the ability to see the larger picture within the smaller scenes of life; acceptance of the greater plan that is made for us. This chakra also displays our ability to let go of damaging thoughts such as envy, greed, obsessions, and painful memories which can hinder the true power of our inner being. It allows us to see how a person with a negative mind harms those around him. The sixth chakra is the sight of the spirit.

Because it contains issues of mental processes this chakra naturally involves the power of the mind, and as such it can create and influence its own reality. If we believe we are helpless pawns moving toward an inevitable destiny then powerless we shall be, vulnerable to everything negative that can pass during our lifetime. In other words, the way you perceive your reality is actually the reality you help to create. Negative thoughts resonate within a low energy level thus attracting negative occurrences within the same energy plane.

This too is true with regard to the health of our physical bodies. The sixth energy center contains the power to enhance health or destroy it through our own attitudes and belief systems. As I mentioned in Chapter 3, how we perceive our world has a profound influence on the health of our physical bodies by altering the flow of vital energy. Recall from Chapter 3 how the mind with its inhibiting perspective initiates imbalance of the spirit, which then causes physiologic changes in the body. These physiologic changes, over time render you vulnerable to the development of illness and disease. If spiritually repressive attitudes and beliefs persist despite the soul's inherent quest for wisdom then this energy center can become distorted. Reflected therein will be the soul's inability to see truth. Denial and lack of insight are also contributory. Chronic headaches, migraine attacks, sinus problems, and learning disabilities may all be related to dysfunctional energy flow in this center.

Empowering our children through truth: By far the most important thing to communicate to our children in relation to this chakra is the magnificent power of their mind. Regardless of the skin they were born in and despite any disabilities they may have, whatever they can envision themselves doing can undoubtedly be achieved. What a child can realize in their lifetime is limitless, especially if it is consistent with the inherent strengths of his incredible inner being.

Mattie T.J. Stepanik was a New York Times bestselling poet and peacemaker who wrote poetry and short stories since the age of three. He has touched the lives of many nationwide with his profound messages of love, peace, courage, and universal love. Astonishingly he was only eleven when his work was first published. Yet he wrote these beautiful pieces while a rare form of muscular dystrophy ravaged his little body. Sadly, Mattie died from this horrific disease only a short time later at the age of thirteen. I mention this little boy and his wonderful achievements as an example of the boundless power of mind and soul. Mattie's inner being was one of a peacemaker, wise far beyond the age of his body. His mind and soul were aligned and as such it expressed an intelligence, vision, and higher awareness that demonstrated the strength and beauty of his spirit, not the confines of his physical body.

Every child, every human, possesses this wisdom which is the wisdom of their *soul*. It is simply a matter of to what degree we can readily access this knowledge and vision. In order to allow this perspective we must strip away the illusions of life which can initiate imbalance of energy in the first place. Examples are materialism and the placing of value on things acquired. We must teach them that true value depends on what lies inside an individual and what they can contribute to the betterment of our existence, and not necessary in what they own. It is equally important to impart the significance of establishing harmony between the heart and mind centers. For it is desirable to lead life with an open heart but important to approach its ups and downs with wisdom, not mere cognition.

Indeed, simply becoming aware of life's illusions is a hard thing to do. Just think about all the gadgets of efficiency we have in this society and how it has bred a faster paced population who expect immediate results and gratification. We have lost sight of nature and God's course of creation. Diminishing, is our use of intuition to help us navigate through the path of life and the common sense of the *soul*. All for the sake of keeping up with the pace that our society has produced. Yes, we as providers of guidance for our children have our very own challenges. We need to take a step back now and then and consult with our inner being. In trying to keep up with this hurried pace what are we losing sight of? And in the process of keeping up are we collecting beliefs and attitudes that contradict truth and inhibit deeper consciousness? We must at times reflect on the thoughts that have proven to be meaningless and devoid of a sense of inner growth and expansion. For this will not serve us in helping our children's inborn purpose for spiritual growth, and it may contribute to a personal and deep sense of being unfulfilled as we age.

Chakra 7 - Crown: This last chakra swirls just atop our head and feeds energy down into our being. The crown center contains our interpretation of a Greater Power and how we apply Its existence to our lives. It is our conscious connection to God, or lack of it. Reflected is our personal search for meaning in this world, our sense of unity with divine creative energy.

As we come to realize the knowledge within the six other energy centers of our inner being there is an awakening in the physical realm to the truths of our existence. No longer do we confuse worship with dictatorship, God's will with human will, and external power with internal power. We also understand the purpose of life and no longer blame God for every hardship that comes along our way. We recognize the power of prayer and the reality of miracles everyday. In other words, we finally get it; it all makes exquisite sense.

Empowering our children through truth: It then goes without saying that to help our children realize this truth we simply teach the spiritual aspect of their being, that eternal part of themselves that unites all as creations of a Higher Being. It is this consciousness that holds the answer to the true meaning of life. Perhaps in teaching them this truth we can help them avoid a point in life which many of us have or maybe have yet to reach; a time of desperately seeking the answer to why they were born and what is the true purpose of existing in this world.

Imparting spirituality to our children can help them in realizing that we all are essentially a group of eternal beings sharing this point in time for the development of both ourselves and humankind. It is up to us how far we can go, as individuals, and as a group. Becoming aware of this consciousness illuminates the truth of how one individual, no matter how small, can affect all of humankind. Like that pebble tossed into a pond where its wake can be felt throughout the body of water.

Encourage acts of kindness every chance you get, and explain the precious worth of the deed. When our children understand and live the truth of this energy center, random acts of kindness may subsequently come easily. For inside they know that they are contributing to something far greater than just that act; they are contributing to a positive energy that will undoubtedly resound in their inner being. A priceless gift which will certainly someday return to them, whether in physical body or not, during this lifetime or the next.

Chapter Six

Sacrificial Development, Balancing, and

Other Spiritual Dynamics

"The important thing is this: To be able at any moment to sacrifice what we are for what we could become."

Charles Duboise

* Samantha had just turned nine months old when she suddenly got sick with what seemed like the common cold. A stuffy nose, occasional cough, and slight fever began early in the evening just before dinner. Because Samantha was *Sharon's first child, she quickly called her mother to ask her opinion of what to do. Her mother, a licensed practical nurse (LPN), advised her to call her pediatrician to get the proper dosage of acetaminophen so the baby would be more comfortable and her fever could be reduced. For the stuffy nose and cough, a vaporizer might do the trick. As soon as Sharon hung up the phone with her mother she called their pediatrician's after-hour's telephone service. While she and her husband waited for the doctor to call back they noticed their daughter was getting rapidly sicker. She began vomiting and her fever escalated to 103 degrees F. Forty five minutes after the initial call the doctor finally phoned them back. Sharon, very worried at this point, insisted that something was terribly wrong with Samantha, and wanted her to be seen immediately by a physician. However her pediatrician asserted that all Samantha had was a nasty upper respiratory infection, that it was "going around this time of year" and to simply give her one teaspoon of acetaminophen and a cool mist vaporizer during sleep. He insisted that a trip to the local emergency department was completely unnecessary. As Sharon and her husband did exactly what the pediatrician instructed she fought becoming panicked over her little girl's increasing lethargy.

Forty minutes later. Sharon thought, shouldn't the medicine be lowering her daughter's fever by now?

Samantha's fever was still 103 degrees and she was so lethargic she could barely keep her eyes open. Sharon called the doctor's telephone service again. This time her husband spoke to the pediatrician, because she was too nervous to even speak. Her husband clearly described Samantha's condition, the persistent fever, the lethargy, the occasional vomiting. The doctor maintained Samantha's case was not an emergency, that they might add a small dosage of ibuprofen to help reduce the fever. He went on to explain that these severe colds are caused by viruses and that the treatment is strictly supportive. Treatment easily provided in the comfort of one's home, not in a the stressful ER of a hospital.

So they gave their daughter more fever reducing medicine and waited. As midnight approached and she held her baby's limp body Sharon cried to her husband that she *knows* something is very wrong with Samantha, that she simply must take her to the hospital despite what the pediatrician told them. Seven hours after the initial contact with their pediatrician they were in their local hospital's ER. Immediately after being triaged, Samantha was whisked off to a room where hospital staff frantically worked on her. Intravenous lines were inserted, oxygen was administered, x-rays were taken, then sonograms of her abdominal area. Specialists were being paged, and many practitioners talked among themselves about their daughter as Sharon and her husband stood in complete and utter disbelief of the terrifying circumstance they were suddenly in. Despite asking every few minutes no one seemed to know for certain exactly what was wrong with baby Samantha; all they knew was that she was now fighting for her life.

Samantha never won that fight, she died that early morning approximately sixteen hours after first becoming ill, of sepsis due to an infection that ravaged her little body. It was only after an autopsy performed on Samantha that a rare congenital disorder was discovered, aslenia. Samantha had been born without a spleen to help her body fight the invasion of germs.

What could possibly be gained from the loss of a child? I share the opinion of most when I assert that there is no emotional pain greater than experiencing the death of your child. It appears completely and utterly senseless. Why would God allow a young and innocent life to leave this world so soon after it arrived? No matter what takes their life, disease or accident, how could He be so cruel?

Let us go back to that celestial scene where the unborn child is contemplating the needs of her own soul. Her Guide, the powerful entity who serves as a beloved mentor, and she reflect on the maturation and wisdom she has achieved so far. The choices and actions from all prior embodied experiences are reviewed. However, there is an upcoming opportunity to share a time and space with a much loved soul peer whose spiritual development is in need of assistance from someone. Someone who loves her so much that she is willing to forsake her own physical life so that the other can experience a spiritual growth like nothing else can promote. She and her guide know exactly what is involved, yet she is ready to demonstrate the most loving act for her soul peer.

Fast-forward in "time" and we may find a case scenario like Sharon and Samantha's. As painful and seeming senseless as it appears, could it be possible that Samantha sacrificed her own short physical life for the soul of her beloved mother? We must pause and reflect on the true meaning of new life. We must re-examine how the precious child in your life will undoubtedly be a soul companion, one you will likely share the *most powerful* relationship during this lifetime within terms of achieving spiritual wisdom and progression. But how can the devastating demise of a child help either to achieve this?

Allow me to elaborate and conclude my story of Samantha's tragic death. All her life Sharon never had much concern over any humanitarian type of issues. She was basically only concerned with what happened within the four walls of her own home, basically because she felt powerless that she could promote change of any kind anywhere. She was also a timid and somewhat insecure woman, easily intimidated by others who she thought knew more than her.

Shortly after Samantha's death, Sharon was compelled to find out more about her daughter's life-threatening disorder. And what she learned shocked her. Most children born with the disorder have some other type of anomaly, an abnormal liver, kidney, or heart. And these anomalies are usually detected either before birth via sonogram or shortly after birth when symptoms quickly arise. Furthermore, if there are any such abnormal organs the disorder can be confirmed by a simple blood smear taken after the baby's birth, and managed aggressively with doses of antibiotics. In Samantha's case she was known to have an abnormal kidney before she was even born. So why was there no diagnostic test performed on Samantha to rule out asplenia? Largely because it is simply not routine follow up. The large majority of children born with aslpenia are diagnosed only after their death via autopsy. And they are likely to die within their first year of life of sepsis caused by a bacteria or virus.

Today, ten years after Samantha's death, Sharon is a fierce advocate for better detection and screening for congenital disorders like asplenia. She has founded an organization that raises the awareness of proper screening and detection for healthcare providers as well as the public. Sharon is no longer the timid woman she used to be, but is now a passionate spokesperson. She and her husband are now also foster parents to four children as well as having two of their own biologically.

I met with Sharon recently and asked her what has changed the most in her life since the tragic loss of her daughter. She replied to me that she cares a lot more about things she never did before. Samantha's death forced her, through sheer anguish and indignation, to become aware of issues she never would have considered before. She now realizes the impoverished and dangerous plight many children are in worldwide, which is why she and her husband became foster parents. And as a result of helping children in need of a home they have so much love in their life from the six children they are now raising. Sharon confided in me that she feels Samantha's presence as though she is still part of the family, and now believes that by leaving her Samantha gave her the precious gift of realizing just how much love she is capable of giving, and the empowerment to exact change in a system she never thought possible. Sharon also said that she has learned to trust her instincts especially when it comes to her children; for she knew within the depths of soul when Samantha was ill she was much sicker than her pediatrician believed her to be. That intimidation, she asserted, would never happen again.

The fact is stories like the one I just told are not uncommon. People who choose to find strength from sorrow, to find a purpose after their tragic loss that enriches their life in some unexpected way that they never thought possible. A part of them that they never knew existed emerges, and takes their life in a direction that promotes the betterment of not only themselves but many others who have shared similar sorrows. Furthermore, some actually say that perhaps the "mission" of their loved one on Earth was accomplished and completed, and that they are now somehow guiding them from the Heavens in their efforts toward such powerful compassion for others. And they often get signs of that guidance; like a favorite item of the deceased mysteriously appears in front of their path, or some other indication that cannot easily be explained. I read recently that a woman who lost her young daughter to skin cancer is now, along with her husband, a determined campaigner for the awareness of how to avoid this deadly disease. She says she often gets signs from her beloved. Throughout her short life her daughter loved sunflowers, and one day after mass as this mother entered her car she noticed one perfect sunflower placed directly in front of her path. She wrote that signs like this happen all the time to her. That she knows in her heart that they are simply her daughter's way of making her support of her parents known.

So, in immersing ourselves in the existence before physical birth, can we somehow comprehend how the "planning from the Heavens" is shaped? Can we see how as cruel and senseless as the demise of a child can be, it can dramatically transform the lives of those that short life touched? Transformation intended for spiritual empowerment and progression. That through unyielding love a soul might sacrifice her own physical being simply to motivate another to expand their soul. Yes, it is extreme; yes, it is unequivocal pain endured. But if strength and compassion does not transpire within the sufferer, can we see how that demise may have been a missed opportunity to truly honor our loved one? Can we, at the very least, sense how our loved one would only want us to progress and move forward with strength and an unembittered heart?

Everyone who is born unto this world has their own "developmental plan" before their physical birth, and that "plan" is continually modified throughout that person's lifetime. Opportunities for growth are carefully laid out in the path of an individual both before and during their life, depending on their human choices when confronted with those opportunities. Again, children do not arrive to this world as a clean slate. They are eternal beings who bring forth an agenda, an intention within a desired arrangement that promotes their growth or the growth of those around them.

All losses of life have the potential to expand or progress those left behind. It is simply an issue of whether or not that was the intent of that soul's arrival to this world. That is what distinguishes sacrificial development. For example, the loss of life can occur in the hands of terrorists, with the hope that progression can come in the form of global intolerance to these acts, and unified steps toward world peace. Loss of life can occur at the hands of Mother Nature, with the faith that the world will show collective compassion for its survivors.

What's more, sacrificial development for the child need not necessarily mean that the outcome be death of his physical body. No, it can also imply a dynamic in which the soul of a child presents a certain challenge for those whose lives he touches. Whether it be via a physical or mental disability, a turbulent disposition or perhaps simply a "different" character from the norm which serves to motivate change, assist us in expanding our perspectives, to move us from stagnation of our inner selves, if you will. Some, in fact, say that this is the purpose of the emergence of the so-called Indigo children (more on that topic in a later chapter). The point is that his spirit arrives primarily with an agenda to assist another entity's progression through extraordinary experiences and trials.

I have a close friend who has learned an exceptional lesson through her second child, one that she speaks about often and to anyone who shares similar experiences with their child. She now understands that what society says is normal behavior may certainly not be seeing the whole picture. And in fact may be missing out on the true beauty of being different. Diane* has two beautiful healthy children, the youngest a boy named Justin*. Since infancy Justin had been very different from her first child. He was a fussy baby unlike his calm sister.

Extremely sensitive to the slightest change in his environment little Justin often was only content in the arms of her mother. When Justin was a toddler he frequently had what is called "night terrors", where he would awaken from sleep in a panic, crying inconsolably, and appearing to be trying to run away from something. When Diane would attempt to comfort her son during these frightening episodes, Justin would seem to be looking right through Diane, not recognizing that it was his mother trying to hold him. Only after a few very long moments, the "spell" that Justin seemed to be in would break, and suddenly he would recognize his mother and allow himself to be embraced. And when asked little Justin could not articulate what was happening to him, or what he was seeing during those scary episodes.

As Justin grew he remained shy and very clingy to his mother. Although her first child and all her friend's children attended some sort of pre-school, Diane sadly knew in her heart that Justin would not cope well with the separation from her and in the unfamiliar setting of school. When not being very clingy to Diane Justin seemed to be a loner, often choosing to play quietly alone as though in his own world. And when he finally had no choice but to start attending kindergarten the school psychologist phoned Diane three weeks into the school year to inform her that all day Justin would cry for her. And that perhaps it would help if Diane gave him a picture of herself to bring to school so that whenever he missed her he could look at his mother's image. Diane described how she broke down in tears after that call from the school psychologist. She questioned why her son needed her so desperately.

And as Justin progressed through the first and second grades school work became more of a challenge. Homework assignments often took hours to complete because Justin would become distracted by the slightest stimuli and have difficulty concentrating on his work. Yet when Justin was tested for learning disabilities his results were negative, suggesting he had none. Diane was determined to have Justin focus on his work in a normal manner like his big sister. But as the frustration mounted so did the arguments, tears, and desperation. Each afternoon Diane would resolve not to get impatient with her son. But as Justin's attention would inevitably begin drifting off his schoolwork Diane's temper would again explode. Ultimately out of sheer frustration Diane would say something she would regret making her darling son dissolve into tears. Gradually, as she watched her son crumble with emotional pain Diane realized that all she was succeeding in was shattering her baby's self-esteem. The moment Diane surrendered to the idea that something was unusual about her sweet son was the moment that she realized his different needs. Diane brainstormed and thought of various strategies to help her son learn, including buying him a voice recorder to help him refocus his thoughts when they drifted. Gradually and steadily Justin was keeping up with his classmates all with the help of his mother's unique tactics.

But there was another side of Justin that seemed to be eclipsed by his differences. Justin was the most thoughtful, tender, caring and intuitive child anyone could know. He easily said the words, "I love you", often and spontaneously to friends and family. He disliked it when anyone spoke negatively about a person, and even spoke up to other children who made fun of others. And he was fantastically intuitive, often knowing what emotions his mother was feeling without so much as looking at her. Diane told me of a time when Justin was sitting on the floor playing alone as usual when Diane began reading a very sad story in a magazine. Not wanting to unnecessarily upset Justin she silently let the tears run down her cheeks as she continued to read the story. Suddenly and without turning to look at her, Justin asked, "Why are you crying, Mommy?" Diane froze. She asked her son how did he know she was crying. Justin simply replied, "I just knew, Mommy." And he got up to hold his mother, only now Diane was crying for more reasons than the sad magazine article. She was so deeply moved by her son's gentle sensitivity.

It was not until Diane began doing some research using the internet that things began to make sense. First she learned that there were varying forms and degrees of the learning disability: Attention Deficit Hyperactivity Disorder. And that unless a child's school performance is significantly impaired that child will not meet the criteria for the diagnosis. According to the description of the sub-disorders Justin appeared to have a mild inattentive type of ADHD without the hyperactivity. Or might the fact that he is easily distracted be a consequence of his keen sensitivity? Furthermore, because he was not falling behind scholastically (primarily due to his mother's ingenuity with specific learning strategies for him) he could not be classified as having this learning disability. Justin was, as all children are, a unique person who could of easily fallen through the cracks of a broad system that does not typically institute individual learning plans. Had it not been for his mother's extraordinary awakening to the specific techniques for her son's learning challenges that desperate afternoon, Justin's difficulties in school would have certainly increased, likely leading to the eventual recommendation of starting medication.

So what were the incredible lessons imparted here? First off, Diane is a changed woman. She is now more aware of how society views things like shyness and learning difficulties and is eagerly trying to promote different reactions to these. Both are referred to in negative terms, as many people expect children to grow up goal-oriented, ambitious, and aggressive in terms of excelling at whatever they undertake. It is especially difficult for boys where sensitivity and lack of aggressive ambition is often teased, lending to that contemptuous name-calling of "sissy" or "pansy", because boys are supposed to be macho. And as far as Justin's high sensitivity and intuitiveness,

Diane watches in awe as he is able to pick up on people's emotions as he walks into a room, or knows exactly when the time is perfect for a hug and a sweet kiss. Diane now sees her son's differences as a blessed lesson to all of those who know him. She wishes that everyone could see the overall good of allowing children like Justin their full expression. And there are many other tender hearted children like Justin who demonstrate profound empathy and thoughtfulness, and have a keen sense of what is cruel, irresponsible, and unjust.

Diane has also learned through her research that Justin's learning difficulties may be tied in to his extraordinary sensitivity. Sensitive children like Justin can become easily aroused or otherwise stimulated. Subsequently, they grow overly anxious and stressed, often leading to trouble with focusing and concentration. This made perfect sense to Diane because Justin had the greatest difficulty with homework when his sister was home either talking on the phone, listening to music or watching TV. The smallest of sounds and happenings around him caught his attention. Once Diane minimized all distracting sounds and activity, he was better able to complete his tasks. And there where other times when all he needed was his mother to sit calmly next to him while he performed his homework. In either case it was, and still is, the tailored approach to his uniqueness that has led to Justin's current success in school.

Diane wonders now if some of the children who are diagnosed with ADHD are simply ones who are very sensitive like Justin. Could countless children be on medication when all they need is sympathetic understanding, a change in their environment, and/or some other creative means to address their finely tuned perceptions? Justin has opened Diane's eyes to an entirely new perspective. What society views as the norm may actually turn out to be a hugely repressive act against the evolution of the human spirit. Seeing the beauty and worth of Justin's sensitivity Diane cannot help but think: what a better world we would live in if these type of differences were better understood and nurtured, as opposed to "corrected" according to some standard. Nowadays whenever Diane hears of a parent struggling with their child's shyness, sensitivity, or lack of concentration she quickly offers to share her insightful perspective of these characteristics. She also communicates with parents the many innovative ways she has learned to help her own child with his extraordinary sensitivity, which often made focusing on tasks a challenge. Diane is currently in the process of launching a discussion group on the benefits of parenting a very sensitive child in her local Mother's Centers. (***For more information on highly sensitive children visit Dr. Elaine Aron's website www.hsperson.com.).

So once again, can we somehow comprehend how the arrival of a child's glorious soul (regardless of any hardship it may bring) can bring about changes where the intention is purely for our progression? Meaning, of course, the expansion of the human soul. Remember this the next time you come upon a "different" child, for it may very well be that those "differences", whatever they may be, are meant to promote change for those around him, or perhaps as grand as society itself. (Thank you Justin).

BALANCING AND OTHER SPIRITUAL DYNAMICS

AFFECTING OUR CHILDREN

For those of you who know the definition of karma, "balancing" has just about the same meaning. I use it instead, because it seems to me more descriptive of the dynamics involved, and I wish to simplify the variations in the definition of the word "karma".

Our Creator made us, all other living beings, and our environment to compliment, harmonize, and balance with one another. The earth provides living beings with sustenance and in turn living beings replenish the earth. If left to its own natural processes the end of something marks the beginning of another; the circle of life, so to speak. Our timeless souls embody that balance, we are a reflective microcosm within the macrocosm of our world. The branches of our lungs provide us with the oxygen needed for our cells, just as the branches of our trees supply that oxygen. Our atmosphere rains down the fluids that sustains the earth, and we in turn pour that down into our bodies for hydration. Our universe contains the Sun which, like our cells, feeds radiant energy to every part of our human tissue.

Recall that energy never dies, it simply transforms. The human body after its demise is transformed into its spiritual state, a state of finer, lighter energy. That energy, which is our spirit, contains a memory or "record" of all embodied life choices. The demise of the physical body does not release any spiritually regressive deeds done during life, it simply carries it now as part of the entity's existence. A type of dooming energy "baggage", you might say, a negative charge that remains as part of your being until balance is restored. The question then becomes, How is balance restored to an individual being who has chosen deeds which act against its progression? The record of energy is simply carried forth to the subsequent lifetime where the opportunity for restoring balance will most certainly exist. Now what might that look like?

Envision this. Choices made during a lifetime include the poor treatment of say, a child, which affects and will be recorded in the second chakra (one on one relationships), among other energy centers. Opportunities for correction and thus growth were not successful. The person passes on without ever really learning the spiritual truth of treating another with honor, and especially a child, with reverence. That distorted energy which indeed contains the "memory" of all actions then carries forth in subsequent lifetimes, until truth is realized. Perhaps that soul chooses to experience similar treatment

93

during his own subsequent lifetime as a means of realizing this truth. In other words, being the victim of acts similar to those he chose to perform during a previous human experience.

The same energy dynamic of spiritual balance may apply toward acts against God's other creations than that of human life. And no, I am not implying that if you mistakenly say, hit a deer while driving on the road, that you are doomed to live out some sort of reciprocal act toward balance. What I am saying, is that if one makes a conscious decision to repeatedly harm, mutilate, or place hateful and ignominious acts against God's living creations without eventually realizing it as wrongdoing, one may create imbalance within his spiritual being which reflects those acts. The divine truths mirrored in the energy centers of our soul may be altered as our Creator lovingly encourages us to achieve reverence toward the environment He designed for us. And what was not realized during one lifetime will be transformed into opportunities for realization during subsequent. In this case, the wonderful truth that as God's creations, we are all connected; and what affects one, will eventually but most certainly, affect us all.

Therefore, as you can see, a newborn baby has an amazing endeavor ahead of her. Her arrival is as courageous as it is miraculous for she brings forth an amazing plan for growth, physically, spiritually, and even universally. Look no more at a child as simply being a biological offspring of an advanced species, for she is far and away much more than the product of union between man and woman. Her skin may be the exact color of her mom's and her eyes may look exactly like her dad's, but the being beneath those eyes and skin is certainly not a creation of that man and woman; that soul is a conception of something far more grand. And she, like each of us, is eternal, having achieved wisdom already from prior experiences. The fact that this particular soul is born into a certain family says that perhaps the family provides either 1) an environment and life circumstance which enhances the opportunity for the soul to mature and progress. Or 2) a shared existence with the entities during which the soul has chosen to aid in the development of those around her. Or 3) an environment which may promote the opportunity for balance otherwise. Time and again you will hear me say that no other human has knowledge of the life "script" that was devised between an individual and our Creator. Of course not, for also within that script human choice is interwoven throughout that person's existence. Therefore, by no means do I imply that this list is exclusive, for as complex, multifaceted, and unique as each being is, so is the extraordinary plan toward her magnificence.

One of my favorite quotes which captures the essence and powerfully transforming event of the sacrificial development of a soul comes from the acclaimed book, *The Cultural Creatives* by Paul H Ray, PH.D and Sherry Ruth Anderson, PH.D. When a woman who had changed her perspective of life and became what the authors call a "Cultural Creative" (a large and growing population of people, with beliefs and lifestyles of enlightenment that involve altruism, self-actualization, and spirituality), she spoke of what prompted these changes in her life. When her son was only five years old he fell victim to a cancer that claimed his life. And as a result, her life was changed in a very dramatic way, propelling her into a life of helping those who are in need in Africa. She went on to describe an image that portrays what she felt at the time, "of a white fire roaring through my life and burning out what was superficial, frivolous, and unimportant and leaving a core of... I don't think there's any other word for it than *love*. A core of love. It's hard to convey what that means."

Just think about how very powerful that is. How, if that was the intention of her son's little soul, to have his mother realize the splendor of that divine truth, what an enormous selfless gift he in fact gave her. There is no measure of that love, and that is the energy that resounds in his mother's spirit

95

for eternity. A realization that love is undeniably, at the core of all. It is the essential ingredient in all that produces joy and a sense of happiness; it is what enriches us all with something far greater than the wealth of our possessions and transcends that which can be seen, heard, or felt. And indeed, it may be that complete and unreserved love we have for our children can have the strength to burn away the illusion that some of us have of what seemingly matters, to what really and truly does.

*Name changed

Chapter Seven

Union of Body and Soul

"It's not nice to fool Mother Nature."

Dr. Robert Bradley

Okay folks, here is where I get a little technical. The science part of my education meets the spiritual side of my understanding of the events which form the conception of a child, as I take you through to the moment of his miraculous birth. It is a glorious journey marked by many external factors that may influence the circumstances in which our beloved arrives to our world.

Human reproductive biology teaches us that conception occurs within the female fallopian tube and that the conceptus embarks on a trip to the uterus for implantation, a process which on the average takes up to ten days. During that time the fertilized cell is rapidly dividing, reaching about a total of one hundred cells at the time of its implantation into the uterus. Once the fertilized cell reaches the uterus and is successfully implanted the woman is considered pregnant. The embryo, if viable, continues to develop into a fetus, a stage which begins around the ninth week of after conception. The embryonic stage however, is the most critical. It is the period where basic structures of all major body organs are completed. Once the embryonic stage has ended the embryo has definite human form and refinements to all systems continue into the fetal period.

In a normal pregnancy birth occurs somewhere between 38 - 42 weeks. A woman's due date is calculated by adding 280 days or 40 weeks to the first day of her last period. Only five percent of babies arrive on their due date; 3 out of 10 babies arrive before and 7 out of 10 arrive after their due date. Birth for first time moms usually occurs after 12 - 14 hours of labor, quicker for experienced moms. The exact mechanism which causes the onset of labor remains a mystery to researchers. What they are certain of however, is that in a normal pregnancy the *baby initiates the process.* Worth repeating, in a normal pregnancy the baby, not your obstetrician, knows when the time is right for its own birth.

The purpose for this abbreviated lesson on the physiology of pregnancy is to provide you with the biological version of birth into the physical world. Now let us once again peer into the realm of the soul and try to view the process from a different perspective. Following the growth and development style of presentation I will guide you through the knowledge I have acquired regarding the physical arrival of a spiritual being. We shall begin this awesome journey with the moment of conception.

The stage is set for our new arrival, the many factors and considerations involved in the initial process of choosing life, which I discussed earlier, are established. Man and woman unite, egg is fertilized and approximately six to ten days later implantation occurs in the uterus. *At the point when the fertilized egg successfully accomplishes implantation the etheric layer of the arriving spirit must merge with the developing embryo or else further physical development is arrested.* Miscarriage or spontaneous abortion would be inevitable if the etheric layer of the unborn child is absent from the womb after implantation.

Recall that the etheric layer of the spirit is the template onto which the developing cells of an embryo and fetus must organize. Without this essential framework the creation of the human body does not continue much beyond actual fertilization; the conceptus is destined to wash away along with a woman's menses days later. With the etheric layer in place the embryo develops into a fetus and continues to grow until birth. Specific genetic information is present in the baby's developing cells, however it is the etheric layer which executes their differentiation.

Once the fetus is physically formed and birth is nearing the spirit, in its entirety, begins its gradual decent into the mother's uterus. (See illustration 7.1). The higher and finer energies of the soul are gently pulled toward the physical body of the baby via an "etheric thread" which resembles something like an umbilical cord. The process of the spirit's decent is intended to be a slow and peaceful one occurring throughout the period of gestation. The complete union of body and soul is a profound event which may occur anywhere between two months to several seconds before birth; the average being more between two weeks and several hours. The spirit as a whole does not spend a significant amount of time in utero because the physical body of the baby is essentially in a state of rest, utilizing energy for physical genesis not unlike the state of sleep.

The completion of a spirit's entrance into the physical body seems to correspond with the unexplainable phenomenon many pregnant women experience before birth called the "nesting urge". Nesting urge is labeled as such to describe a woman's sudden mysterious desire to clean and otherwise prepare the home for her baby's impending arrival. I believe the nesting urge is sparked by the woman's own inner being sensing the moment her baby's complete essence merges with body within her. Pregnant mammals also display it. This impulse of spiritual origin is very real and strong; it is no wonder why science and its study of the *physical* world can not explain what causes it.

First Trimester	Second Trimester	Third Trimester
Physiological Course of Pregnancy:	**Physiological Course of Pregnancy:**	**Physiological Course of Pregnancy:**
Sperm and egg unite, egg travels down the fallopian tube of the female and embeds itself in the uterine lining, a process called "implantation". If implantation is successful, human cells continue to multiply and differentiate, organizing the systems of the physical body. Fetus resembles a miniature human being by the end of this trimester	The fetus is growing rapidly and gaining weight. All physical systems are in place including a beating heart, an intact nervous system, eyes that can see, and ears that can hear	Final refinements are made in the nervous, sensory, cardio-respiratory, and integumentary (skin and hair) systems. Rate of growth slows as full term approaches.
Spiritual Happenings:	**Spiritual Happenings:**	**Spiritual Happenings:**
Etheric layer of the spiritual body of the baby must merge with the fertilized egg by the time of implantation into the uterine lining. If this does not occur, further development is arrested and spontaneous abortion (miscarriage), is inevitable. Once etheric layer is in place, it acts as a grid or framework whereby human cells differentiate and physical development occurs.	The higher, finer energies of the baby begin their slow decent to unite with the slower and denser energy of the etheric layer. The presence of the complete spiritual body of the baby is not needed during this time of gestation as the physical body is basically in a state of rest. He/she is essentially utilizing energy for physical genesis.	In a normal pregnancy body and soul, in its entirety, unite sometime during this trimester. It is a profound moment where many women sense its occurrence, an event I believe corresponds with the "nesting instinct".

As I mentioned earlier, the union of physical body and soul should be a slow, gentle transition. Now allow me to assist you in imagining for a moment that you can remember your very own process of coming into "being". You, as an entity of luminous energy, are at "home", surrounded by unconditional love and beauty, and unencumbered by anything of the physical world.

100

You exist without pain or worldly worries. You know that all is fair and good, that none of God's creations can escape the consequences of its own actions or choices, and that the goal for visiting "school Earth" is to allow your spirit to grow and develop through human experience. Now imagine, after much counsel and contemplation with your spiritual guides and/or teachers, the time has come for you to once again incarnate. Your goals for progression are laid out, yet you know once you are in physical form you will not remember them, or much of anything else having to do with your true "home". You are excited or apprehensive, or a combination of both. Your guide(s) lovingly encourage you, letting you know they will be with you every step of the way, even though you may not always be aware of them.

Your once weightless form is now being slowly pulled into dense, heavy matter. You are startled by the new sounds and sensations which bombard you while in the womb, but you allow yourself to gradually get used to them. You know enough to brace yourself for the physical stress of birth itself. And when you are totally ready, you signal the body and energies of your biological mother to begin the process of your arrival.

In contrast, imagine having no control. Having to immediately transition to body, no time for acclimation or preparation. You are commanded into the physical world at someone else's authority. Hardly an image of the tranquil journey you so desperately need, yet one many newborns must endure in this day and age of "convenience child-birthing".

During gestation, the **etheric** layer of the spiritual body is present providing the "template" onto which the cells of a developing fetus organize. The higher and finer energies of the baby begin their slow decent to unite with the slower and denser energy of the etheric layer. In a normal pregnancy, body and soul, in its entirety, unite sometime during the third trimester. When union is complete (or near complete), only then will **baby** initiate her own birth.

A Sign of Our Times: Controlling Nature's Process of Birth

In keeping with our society's current and prevailing thinking the process of birth should, of course, too be a controlled event. Why not, physicians reason. Body is bio-machine and they are the skilled mechanics of that structure. Why not streamline the process of birth so that it is both convenient and cost-effective. (Cost-effective in terms of avoiding malpractice claims.) And while we are at it, let us praise the perks of a controlled birth.

* You can be certain to have your practitioner of choice at the delivery (Dr. X will or will not be on call the weekend of your due-date).

* You can choose your child's birth date, (a little shaky of the number 13? Let's schedule that birth for the 12th!).

* Afraid of a little urinary incontinence after vaginal birth? No problem! We'll schedule a cesarean section so that you won't have to push your baby out and risk stretching those muscles.

* Want to make it to your sister's wedding with enough postpartum time to get back into shape? Easy! We'll schedule the birth the minute you're thirty-eight weeks.

I can go on and on. While working as a nurse on a maternal/child unit, I cannot count how many incidents I knew of where a doctor and/or their pregnant patient chose to schedule the birth of a baby either by induction of labor or cesarean section. Sometimes it was for the convenience of the doctor, other times for the patient. I have heard many women complain that they could not endure their pregnancy a day longer, and demand that their physician hasten their baby's arrival by inducing labor. Some opt for elective c-section, worried that they will become incontinent of urine if they deliver their baby vaginally. Then there were the times when I have been in the operating room where the reason stated for a cesarean was that the doctor suspected the woman was carrying a large baby and could not naturally give birth, only to later deliver a six and a half pound newborn. I think the most startling reason I have heard of was a woman who wanted to put a halt to her widening girth, and even more shocking, her doctor obliged by inducing her labor at the start of her baby's 38th week of gestation.

Then, of course, I knew of women who, because they had a long, hard labor for their first child, were afraid of repeating a similar experience, and therefore chose an elective cesarean section. Please do not misunderstand me. I am not trivializing the genuine fear some women have over the event of childbirth, especially if their first experience was anything less than wonderful. However, I do believe that a woman should avoid making her decision on scheduling the birth of her baby based on previous experience, or the experiences of others. Just as every pregnancy is unique so is every birth. A labor that lasted over twenty-four hours the first time may only be two hours for the next pregnancy.

In fact, I know of many women, both personally and professionally, who have had dramatic differences in their birth experience from one child to their next. The fundamental issue seems to be the *tools* women have accessible to help them through the process of ushering new life into this world. You see, the body and soul know what has to be done, involuntarily and instinctively. The physical aspect of it is, under normal circumstances, an autonomic event. A woman who is in a coma can give birth naturally to a baby without any medical intervention. Likewise, a healthy woman who is left to her own devises can tune in to the ancient wisdom of her female spirit, and intuitively move and position her body in ways that facilitate the birth of her baby.

Oftentimes, what becomes the obstacle for women to give birth in a natural and healthy manner is the power of the mind over the body and soul. Fear of pain, anxiety over the unknown, and the worrying about everything from the health of the newborn to the loss of control, all render the mind a very powerful influence over the body and soul. The body then tenses and constricts inhibiting the smooth release of our precious baby. The soul is quieted and cannot speak to its physical form about what position or action to take that will ease the journey of its inhabitant. Tools, whether they be enlisting the support of a doula, utilizing the cognitive techniques of Hypno-Birthing, or relying on acupuncture for pain control all have a similar common goal. Modifying how a woman will perceive the experience of birth. In reducing the anxiety and fear we allow the body unobstructed permission to perform its awesome work, and the soul an elevated voice to intuitively assist in this most miraculous passage.

We may augment the natural process of birth by participating in the very real practice of sensing and communicating with the essence of your unborn child. A process I will guide you through in Chapters 9 and 10. By heightening your intuition you will be increasing your responsiveness to the cues your baby gives you as she nears her own birth. In perceiving your baby's signals, you may be able to intuitively know when birth is imminent; you may even have the capacity to influence your baby's safe arrival. In Chapter 10, I will provide specific exercises on how pregnant women can enhance their intuition and move the energy of their body in preparation for birth.

My sister had three pregnancies. Her first pregnancy was normal, however her labor lasted twenty-nine long, grueling hours. Her second child was in a breech position (feet first) in her last trimester, and her physician attempted to turn the baby while still in her uterus during her eighth month of pregnancy. My sister went into labor ten days after her due date. After twelve hours of strong contractions her daughter started showing signs of fetal distress (decreased heart rate as a result from reduced oxygen supply). Initially unaware that the baby was still malpositioned it became apparent to the healthcare team that child could not safely pass vaginally. My sister ended up needing a cesarean section after enduring many hours of powerful contractions and emotional worry over the safety of her unborn daughter.

By the time my sister became pregnant with her third child she was understandably apprehensive about giving birth. She had a normal, worry-free pregnancy but as her due date approached her anxiety increased. Six days after her due date she was ready throw in the towel. She asked her physician to schedule the delivery of her baby anticipating she may need, or even want, a cesarean section.

It was during this time that I had begun studying the practices of Eastern medicine. I was particularly intrigued with energy medicine as I had learned that many of my nursing colleagues used the practice as an adjunct to traditional medicine. I spent about ten minutes moving the energy of her body with my hands, focusing on clearing and opening her root chakra which would in turn facilitate the opening of her cervix. While I was doing this my sister reported seeing a deep red swirling vortex shape in her mind's eye. The vortex was cloudy at first but as I moved the energy of her root chakra she claimed it got clearer and its center widened. I continued moving my hands over her body for about ten minutes. My sister gave birth to my niece six hours later, after only two hours of labor.

Again, I am speaking of normal pregnancies. Obviously this would not apply to the woman who, as an example, has a narrow pelvic outlet making a normal vaginal delivery impossible. And I am certainly not saying that if there is a situation which may compromise the health or safety to either mother or child that medical intervention should be avoided. Quite the opposite; often in emergency situations the impending danger is in part the result of the essence needing to be born in an immediate manner. An example of this is the medically necessary cesarean section for a fetus who is not tolerating a particularly long and stressful labor. Or any situation which places the pregnancy in a high-risk category such as pre-eclampsia, gestational diabetes, or placenta previa (placenta at opening of cervix), to name a few. The difference in these cases usually lie with the biological *mother's* condition of health before and/or during her pregnancy. When a problem with pregnancy exists oftentimes the baby's soul, knowing this, is prepared to be born with the help of medical intervention. It is my firm belief that God often works through the hands of healthcare professionals at times when things go wrong. However, research has shown when intervention occurs outside of medicinal reasons, bypassing this perfect process of nature leads to *less* control over the birth of a baby.

As stated earlier, under normal circumstances baby initiates his own birth. That is the natural course of childbirth. Studies have proven that labor inductions can produce more painful contractions and *longer* labors, (average lasting 24-36 hours). As a result more medical interventions become necessary such as the use of epidurals, electronic fetal monitoring, Foley (bladder) catheterizations, and ultimately a 50%-250% chance of having a cesarean section because of induction failure. Recent studies have shown that cesarean sections have increased from 20 percent in 1996 to an all time high of 27 percent in 2002. And the numbers continue to rise. The major risk involved to the baby from elective inductions is fetal distress resulting from uterine hyperstimulation (abnormal rhythm and strength of contractions), umbilical cord compression, and infection. Babies with increased incidence of neonatal jaundice and low Apgar scores upon birth have also been documented.

Cesarean sections save lives, no one, of course, will dispute that fact. Millions of women and babies survive what would otherwise be tragic birth experiences because of this marvelous medical advantage. Furthermore, I share the belief with many that medical advancement is an integral part of spiritual progression, in terms of inner desire to alleviate human suffering. However, c-sections are intended to be an emergency intervention for the safety of mother and child. This procedure is considered major abdominal surgery. One that carries with it undesirable outcomes such as risk of infection, longer hospital stays, post-operative pain, and a much lengthier recovery which often interferes with a woman's ability to adequately feed and nurture her baby during the postpartum period. All of which again, would certainly be worth it if it meant the safe outcome of mother and baby.

Yet labor inductions are so common these days under the deceptive lure of control and convenience. Again, 50%- 250% of labor inductions end up with the pregnant woman having to undergo a c-section. Are these numbers and outcomes merely a case of *irony*? That they mean nothing significant because science says it knows when a baby can be born? I do not think so. Simply put, although 38 weeks gestation is considered full term, in a healthy pregnancy, baby may not be ready to be born. Inductions may not go smoothly because baby has not yet signaled her mother to begin labor.

But at what point in her physical development does a baby naturally initiate her own birth? When is she ready to enter our world on her own terms? Indeed the initiation of labor is a mystery that plagues medicine to this day; for it is also an important part in understanding and preventing premature births. (More on complications of pregnancy in the next chapter.) However, I believe that in a healthy pregnancy, initiation of birth occurs in part when the baby's spiritual body, that distinct inner being of every human, has completed his journey of uniting with that of his physical. Spirit has joined with body and has just begun its elusive, and often lifetime, task of complete integration with the mind. Only then does the healthy unborn fetus trigger a set of physiologic responses in his mother via excretion of powerful hormones that enable him to exit his uterine home. Once body and soul are united, the actual birth is under the control of the baby's soul but is not without significant influence. There are many elements, both natural and not, which become a factor in determining a baby's specific time of birth. It can be influenced by the cyclic energy of the Earth, decisions of healthcare workers, and maternal stress, just to name a few. The important point here is that when the process of birth in a normal pregnancy is not *triggered* by the baby (as evidenced by events like cervical dilation >3cm., rupture of membranes, intensification of contractions, etc.), the transition of soul to body may be particularly stressful. The spirit must be able to adjust to the drastically denser matter of the body, which is no simple feat. And though the vast majority of infants tolerate scheduled births well, it is an added stress which I am sure they would fare far better without.

Conception marks the coming of a precious soul to our world. Full of promise with an agenda intended for betterment, our new arrival is both exquisitely courageous and beautifully hopeful for all of us sharing her time here. May we honor our child's arrival and allow her soul peaceful union with her physical body when nothing threatens. Doing so will likely ensure a birthing experience in which the Heavens collaborated with.

Chapter Eight

When Something Goes Wrong With Fetal Development

"In the middle of every difficulty lies opportunity."
Albert Einstein

Can anyone argue how truly magnificent the development of an unborn baby is? An abbreviated fashion of the details I presented in the last chapter go something like this: sperm fertilizes egg, egg rapidly divides into what resembles an ocean-dwelling shrimp by the fourth week of gestation, and by the eighth week this remarkable conception contains all its body systems in place, including a beating heart, and takes the form of a small human. The rest of the thirty-something weeks is spent refining those body systems until this miraculous creation initiates its own birth into the world. With as much complexity that is involved it is an absolute medical wonder in itself that the vast majority of babies born are normal and healthy.

And indeed there are many things within the scope of the human existence that science may try, but cannot explain. Ask any veteran doctor who has seen her share of the unexplainable during her years of practicing medicine, and she will have to admit there indeed exists a mystifying area of unknown. It is the same domain where physicians are held powerless and medical miracles occur. It is that territory where life and death are commanded by something far greater than human intelligence and skill. This is the realm of the spirit, the only one where new life

111

can lovingly be created and ushered in this world.

Once the creation of new life is underway, the normal and healthy development of a baby consists of an intimately intricate dance between the physical and spiritual bodies of mother and baby. Physically, it in part involves the enormous power of hormones and the structure and function of the maternal body. Spiritually however, it encompasses the subtle energies of the mother, and the basic integrity of the unborn child's etheric layer. Recall from Chapter Two that it is the etheric layer of the spirit that serves as a template of energy onto which the dividing cells of the fetus organize. Problems that can arise during pregnancy, birth, or with the health of the newborn may have its origins within the dynamics of their spiritual bodies. Energy dysfunction from mother, baby, or perhaps even both. Let me explain.

Pregnancy-induced hypertension, hyperemesis gravidarum (severe and uncontrollable vomiting which may persist beyond the first trimester, and lead to serious health consequences for mother and unborn baby), and pre-term labor are just a few complications of pregnancy of which doctors cannot readily identify a cause. The origin of certain congenital disorders are just as mysterious, having no risk factors to foresee their development, such as the exposure to a teratogen that would predict fetal anomalies. And although no one can profess omnipotent knowledge of why certain happenings occur in life I do want to provoke your contemplation on some possible factors when it comes to prenatal outcomes. My intention is to have you consider the roles and interactions of our dynamic inner being with our mind in influencing the structure and function of the physical body. Perhaps when taken into account certain mysteries obscuring the normal or abnormal course of pregnancy and birth of a child will be illuminated. And maybe then treatments that holistically address the individual will become a standard in our attempts of achieving healthy outcomes for mom and baby.

HOLISTIC ASSESSMENT: MOTHER

Holism: the theory and practice of addressing all aspects of a person's life during the healing process; the mental, emotional, social, and spiritual conditions, not just physical symptoms, are taken into account throughout the treatment of illness. Makes perfect sense, right? Especially in light of all the recent studies that suggest a strong link between life circumstance and the development of a certain disease. Heartache and loneliness linked to cardiac troubles, immune suppression and impaired neurological function linked to a person's refusal to forgive others. Women who are unhappy at work (outside the home) are two times more likely to develop heart disease. And married women who avoid conflicts with their husbands by silencing themselves are four times more likely to die *of any cause* compared with those who openly show their feelings. I can go on and on because it seems as though almost everyday there is new evidence supporting the mind, body, soul connection. Traditional medicine is finally proving to themselves what eastern medicine has known for centuries. Empower yourself to know what makes for true health and well-being throughout *all* of your life, for yourself and for those you love .

"Complimentary", or "alternative" treatments as it is often referred to, are outside of the traditional approach of the field of medicine and are methods of helping a person heal. Biofeedback and guided imagery are well known methods used within the therapeutic professions. They provide excellent examples of how altering your thoughts can bring about positive changes in the body. Meditation is simply a spiritual variation of these, accomplishing focused thought by either oneself or in a meditation group. Other forms of complimentary treatment include things like homeopathy, hypnosis, aromatherapy, and therapeutic massage, just to name a few. One type of method includes treatments which address the subtle energies of the body,

113

aptly termed "energy work" or "energy medicine". Energy work includes the techniques of acupuncture, acupressure, cupping, Reiki, Therapeutic Touch, Hands-on Healing; and to some degree the meditative type of exercises like Yoga and Tai Chi. Many of these practices are perfectly safe during pregnancy and are in fact praised by those who utilize them. I will provide a comprehensive list of those that are safe later on in this chapter.

When I was a student in nursing school I had the fortunate experience of witnessing the power of complimentary treatments early in my prospective career. It was during my home care practicum that I met *Samantha, a twenty-eight year old who was twenty weeks pregnant and had severe hyperemesis. Day and night, Samantha suffered from nausea and would vomit just about anything she would put in her mouth. She had recently been discharged from the hospital with an order for home care nursing to closely monitor for dehydration and other dangers for mom and baby which may arise from persistent vomiting. As a student, my responsibility was to follow her primary nurse and learn the ever-important role of home care nursing in our communities. To my benefit I learned quite more.

This was Samantha's first pregnancy. And although she had determined she would be a single parent she was not without the natural ambivalence about her decision and her upcoming challenges. She was also very anxious about what could go wrong during the birth of her child. Unfortunately, she had a couple of friends who had negative experiences with their deliveries (incidentally, both had labor inductions), and they wasted no time in telling her all the painful details. It was the job of the home care nurse to not only medically monitor Samantha, but to also educate her on the processes of pregnancy and childbirth.

Approximately two weeks after starting our home care visits to Samantha we began noticing a dramatic change in both her physical and mental status. She reported that she had not vomited in the past two days and had minimal nausea. Her physical assessment showed nothing abnormal. But perhaps what was more striking was that she was also more relaxed, calmer, and claimed to have more energy than she has ever had in the past twenty-one weeks of her pregnancy. Samantha's primary nurse suspiciously asked right away, "Okay, Samantha, what gives?"

It turned out that one day while Samantha was in the hospital, a volunteer worker approached her to ask if she was interested in reading the daily newspaper. After refusing the offer, the woman continued talking to Samantha, eventually asking why she was in the hospital. Becoming somewhat annoyed at this woman, she abruptly told her about the medical problems. The woman then did not hesitate in handing her a card with the name of a licensed Acupuncturist. The woman swore that the practitioner would indeed help, that she only need to give it a try.

And try she did. Samantha reported having immediate results, particularly after the Acupuncturist placed his needles in a location two fingers above the inner wrist. Surprisingly her stomach felt calm and her mind tranquil. And the night of her first treatment she had the most restful sleep she had had since learning she was pregnant. After receiving several Acupuncture treatments, Samantha told her primary nurse and I that she was also less anxious about the pregnancy, and spoke optimistically for the first time about her impeding birth and motherhood. Having met her health goals Samantha was soon discharged from home care nursing services. Although I no longer had the opportunity to follow her pregnancy I was certain that with her new outlook she would manage just fine.

So what kind of miracles did the Acupuncture impart on Samantha? How was it that this non-traditional treatment dramatically improved the outcome of Samantha's complicated pregnancy and in the process touched her mind and spirit?

Acupuncture is an ancient practice of Chinese medicine involving the insertion and manipulation of needles in as many as 2000 points of the human body, depending on the specific treatment. These points are mapped out along meridians or pathways where the vital energy of our body runs. Chinese refer to this vital energy as Qi (pronounced "Chee"). Qi is a direct reflection of the essential elements of our existence, the spiritual, emotional, mental, and physical aspects of our lives. Blockages, stagnation, or leakages along these meridians indicate the imbalance of Qi. If imbalance of Qi occurs it is believed that the universal forces which also nourish the body become altered, making the physical body vulnerable to illness and disease.

Because the flow of vital energy is influenced in part by our human experience this imbalance can be caused from inappropriate emotional responses, such as excessive anger, fear, deep grief, etc. Therefore what may emerge are energy distortions created by the secular mind. Maladaptive responses in life which, with its inhibiting perspective, initiates imbalance of the spirit that then causes physiologic changes in the body.

The needles used in Acupuncture act to stimulate, redirect, and reconnect the body's energy force in an attempt to restore balance and thus health to an individual. The fundamental beliefs of Acupuncture are used also with Acupressure (using manual pressure instead of needles), Moxibustion (applying heat to acupressure points), Cupping (applying suction to points), and Reflexology (stimulation of points along the soles of the feet). The ultimate goal being achievement of health by addressing mind, body, and spirit.

Could Samantha's development of hyperemesis gravidarum have had anything to do with her ambivalence about her decision to be a single mom? Could her heightened anxiety regarding the birth of her baby be a factor? Was it possible that her responses to her current life situation subconsciously affected the vital energy of her dynamic inner being? And if so, did the Acupuncture treatments actually restore healthy energy flow throughout her fragile body which held life?

The field of medicine provides demographic profiles of those afflicted with a certain illness, intriguing factors that are often present in the lives of its sufferers. In other words, conventional medicine has found there are certain psychosocial happenings that are more prevalent in those with a particular illness than in those without that illness. Case in point, hyperemesis gravidarum. Research has indicated that it is more common in young women less than twenty years old, during their first pregnancy and where the woman has inadequate information about the pregnancy and/or is overly anxious about the birth. Hyperemesis gravidarum has also been linked to women without a partner, or those who perceive lack of support from their partners. It is seen more in women who have experienced post-traumatic stress disorder, excessive social stress, depression, and anxiety.

The only problem is that it is sometimes difficult to determine which event preceded the other. In other words, is it possible that those factors (anxieties about the birth and the prospect of facing the pregnancy without support of partner) *occurred or were exacerbated* as a result of being ill with hyperemesis gravidarum; or were they present *before* the onset of the illness itself.

Pregnancy-induced hypertension is a potentially fatal disorder (for mom and/or baby) that appears to have certain psychosocial characteristics associated with it as well. It has been found to occur more often in women during their first pregnancy, those of lower socioeconomic status, those with poor access to prenatal care, and those whom have had a recent change in partner or a history of multiple sex partners. Not to mention, of course, those with well known disposition for the disease, such as those of African American decent and those with pre-existing hypertension and cardiovascular disease, (third chakra issues which we touched upon in Chapter 3).

My position is this. Whether the illness or the behavior/emotions/thinking came first really is not the important issue when it comes to fixing the body. What needs to be done immediately is whatever works to make the pregnant woman better physically. Achieved for the most part through close monitoring of physical symptoms, and treatment through the use of medicines. But when it comes to lasting wellness all aspects of an individual's life become instrumental. When you think about it, both scenarios are an issue of perspective. If the behavior/ emotions/ thinking brought the illness on, then it is clearly an issue of that person's perspective of their life events. However, it is still an issue of a person's perspective if the illness brings about stress-related behaviors/ emotions/ thinking, because these factors are known to be characteristics which exacerbate the illness. What *is* critical in terms of enhancing healing of any kind is that all aspects are addressed: mind, body, and soul. The mind is responsible for its perspective on life. Maladaptive responses create imbalance of the soul; imbalance of the soul's energies create physical symptoms. One cannot have lasting health if only the body is healed.

And in *all* cases of illness when the body cannot be healed, well-being of the soul and mind can make all the difference in the world during the end of life. Studies have shown that those with terminal illness experience better quality of life and less depression when they have spiritual beliefs. Mentally they are better able to cope with their diagnosis and are emotionally more content. Research has shown time and again that what proves to bring about health and/or a sense of wellness are the changes a person makes within their entire lifestyle; meaning their physical, emotional, mental, and spiritual lives.

Nausea and vomiting are very common, and in fact reassuring, consequences of a healthy pregnancy. While at this point we can only speculate why it can occur in excessive and dangerous amounts, one must take note of the accompanying behavioral, emotional, and mental factors for any illness as they may hold the key to real healing. Acupuncture may have worked for Samantha simply because it addressed issues within her that medicine was not. Whether through balancing the energy of her body, or by providing a relaxing environment to calm her mind, the end result was improved health for her and her baby. The same can be said of numerous other ailments of pregnancy in which the *mother's* imbalance is the primary source of risk. The Table outlines those complications of pregnancy with their safe complimentary adjuncts toward wellness. *(Any and all treatments during pregnancy, including those considered "natural" should be discussed with your obstetric practitioner. Many treatments should not be utilized during the first three months of pregnancy, as this is an extremely vulnerable time of fetal development.)*

Many complimentary treatments are safe and effective for pregnant women, except for those that require ingesting something such as herbs or plant extracts, any exercise or applied device considered too rigorous or stimulating to the uterine muscle. **These can be very dangerous and should not, under any circumstance, be used at any point during your pregnancy.** A few of the safe complimentary treatments available for pregnant women are:

* **Acupuncture/ Acupressure/ Cupping**: An effective type of Chinese Medicine explained earlier in this chapter. Most states require that practitioners become licensed, and you can find one that is qualified by contacting your State's Education Department and Office of Professions. Also you may want to ask family members and friends who have had experiences with Chinese Medicine so they may be able to recommend a good practitioner.

* **Pre-Natal Yoga:** Effective and safe when guided by a qualified practitioner with expertise in prenatal exercise. Pre-Natal yoga can build strength, flexibility, energy, and increase circulation in a woman's body. It can help with back and leg pain, sore or cramped muscles, and the water retention which causes swelling in pregnancy. Because of yoga's focus on breathing and relaxation, it can promote a more restful sleep and help with the anxiety and stress of pending motherhood. But what I find to be perhaps one of the most glorious benefits of pre-natal yoga is its teachings of moment-by-moment awareness of one's body. This

practice of mindful presence promotes a wonderfully fulfilling experience of pregnancy and birth as you encounter this most phenomenal event.

* **Hands-On Healing:** This type of healing includes the modalities of Therapeutic Touch, Reiki, Bioenergy healing, spiritual healing, and Pranic healing, to name a few. Its focus toward wellness lies in the ability to move, realign, and enhance the body's energies to promote optimal functioning of the physical body. It can help reduce the fatigue, nausea, aches, and pains associated with pregnancy. And because of its ability to put a person in a state of deep relaxation, energy work can calm and soothe both mother and unborn baby, thus reducing the anxiety and stress of upcoming birth. Methods such as Reiki and Therapeutic Touch claim to ease the pain of birth, and helps to create an atmosphere of peace during baby's time of arrival. Finding a qualified practitioner may be simpler these days because many of the modalities now offer certification for their particular practices. So ask your prospective practitioner if she has certification, and again seek those who have been recommended by others

* **Guided Imagery and/or Meditation:** A technique which utilizes the power of the mind- body connection through deep relaxation. Guided imagery can enable a woman to become self-assured, confident, and more in control of her body during the birthing experience. During pregnancy it can help reduce nausea, headaches, as well as other muscle and joint discomforts. And during the birthing event it may reduce the need for pain medications. Those who practice guided imagery during pregnancy also claim to experience immediate and joyful bonding with their baby because of their enhanced control and minimal need for pain intervention.

Meditation, like guided imagery, uses the individual's mind to enter into a state of deep relaxation and connect to their inner being. It is a form of quieting the mind that can be achieved when the mind is unoccupied by formal logic. Perhaps quite encouragingly, a meditative state can be achieved while performing mindless tasks such as housework, taking baths or showers, listening to music, or any other activity that allows your mind to "zone out" and begin an unfolding of thoughts. Capture that moment of streaming thought and allow it to flow in a direction you want it to. Like ways to increase communication with your unborn baby or the bestowal of ancient inner wisdom. Meditation is a simple practice that anyone can do, even during times when you are seemingly "occupied".

* **Aromatherapy**: This is the art of utilizing the scents of essential oils to alleviate many common complaints of pregnancy. Morning sickness, indigestion, stretch marks, fatigue, edema, and muscular cramps are all ailments aromatherapy says it can help.
  Spearmint, lavender, lemon, chamomile, and geranium, used alone or in mixtures, are some of the scents you can inhale to bring about positive results. You must consult a reputable resource on how and what to use for specific ailments; there are many excellent books available. Several sources I drew from though indicate that essential oils from bay leaves, clove, basil, clary sage, sage, marjoram, oregano, thyme, and wintergreen should be avoided by pregnant women as they pose a safety risk.

* **Hypnosis/HypnoBirthing:** Hypnosis has been around for many years and HypnoBirthing is an effective spin-off on the principles of this practice and the works of Dr. Grantly Dick-Read, one of the pioneers in the field of natural childbirth. In general hypnosis is a sort of reprogramming of the mind. This reprogramming can include having the mind believe that birth will be a painless, joyful, and easy event. In fact, hypnosis has been used in lieu of anesthesia with patients who have allergies to these type of drugs.
  HypnoBirthing-The Mongan Method, created by Marie Mongan, M.Ed., M.Hy, specifically teaches expectant parents

how to use only positive views, messages, and expectations of their pregnancy and upcoming birth. By doing so this can replace all fear and anxiety which is known to, among other negative outcomes, create tension which can then create pain. Fear and anxiety have long been known to produce dysfunctional labor, thus increasing the chances of cesarean section. Some of the benefits of HypnoBirthing are: less, or no use of drugs during labor; shorter labors due to enhanced relaxation and freedom from fear; a calm peaceful birthing environment; fewer medical interventions during labor; and malpositioned (ie. Breech) babies may be turned using hypnosis.

Hyperemesis Gravidarum	Pregnancy-Induced Hypertension	Gestational Diabetes	Pre-term Labor
Complimentary Treatments: ***Chinese Medicine Hands-On Healing, (ie. Reiki, TT) Guided Imagery, Aromatherapy Ginger**	Complimentary Treatments: ***Chinese Medicine, Prenatal Yoga, Guided Imagery, Meditation, Hands-On Healing, Hypnotherapy**	Complimentary Treatments: ***Chinese Medicine, Prenatal Yoga, Hands-On Healing,**	Complimentary Treatments: ***Chinese Medicine Guided Imagery, Meditation,**

(* Chinese Medicine refers to the modalities of Acupuncture, Acupressure, Cupping, and Moxibustion. They are listed as one approach because, depending on the ailment, one modality may be safer and more effective than the other. Check with a reputable, qualified Chinese Medicine practitioner and your healthcare provider for specific treatment that is right for you.)

Pregnancy, childbirth, and motherhood are just about the most transformational events that a woman can possibly go through. It touches all parts of her being: mind, body, and unquestionably her soul. And accordingly, when needed, all parts should be supported. Everyday more evidence is pointing to this very real connection in terms of healing and well being. *Be unaware no longer; treatments which address the health of also mind and soul are the most effective when it comes to overall well-being.* And even in cases when the body cannot be fixed, addressing one's spiritual needs alone can significantly improve the quality of life.

Holistic Assessment: Baby

Never shall I assume to have knowledge of why a certain child is born with the challenges of potentially fatal disorders. For as I have said numerous times before, I believe no human has the script of life created between an individual and his Creator. I have however, in the previous chapters offered the possibilities in terms of spiritual progression. Perhaps those infants who visit our physical world for only a brief period of time do so primarily for those whose lives they touch. For it would be logical to conclude that little or no opportunity for *self* development would occur.

In the most basic sense I see fetal development as having both afferent and efferent influence. Recall how I use these terms, afferent meaning "bringing toward the body", and efferent meaning "directing or bringing out from the body". Afferent influence on the developing embryo and later fetus includes such things as genetic programming from the biological parents. Embryonic cells assemble, divide, and differentiate on the framework of the etheric field. Let us assume for a moment that the etheric field is healthy and intact, but the cells developing on it have genetic material which has a disorder programmed within them. The baby will unfortunately grow to have these diseased cells within its physical body. Traditional medicine is used as an attempt to "fix" the physical body. Complimentary treatments in a young infant can work to strengthen the body's flow of energy so that optimal support for healing can occur. Or it can be used to curtail some of the side effects of the traditional therapy, such as anxiety, nausea, or pain. Nevertheless, the disease that develops is a result of afferent causes during fetal development; "faulty" biological programming of the cells being laid down upon the etheric field.

Conversely, *efferent* influence consists of disorder programmed within the etheric field itself. In other words, the soul brings forth to physical life recorded issues or traumas within its spiritual being.

Recall from Chapter 6 that the human energy contains a memory or "record" of all embodied life choices. And how the demise alone of the physical body does not release any spiritually regressive deeds done during life, that it simply carries it now as part of the entity's existence. I described it as a type of dooming energy "baggage", a negative charge that remains as part of your being until balance is restored. It is that same energy that can cause disease promoting imbalance, energy distortions present even before birth. For it is part of that individual's issues toward his own progression. It is this type of imbalance that traditional medicine usually cannot cure. The only ways in which *it may* (I say "may" because that individual's life script may already have its predetermined ending) be halted is through correction or alteration of the spiritual issues which have caused the imbalance in the first place.

On the other hand, recorded *trauma* within the etheric field is slightly different. Still a type of efferent energy dysfunction it arises from traumatic experiences that the entity underwent while in previous physical form. Usually it is what caused its physical death. Say for example, a child is born blind. That blindness may have been the result of recorded trauma to the etheric field of that being when he, say, perished because of a fatal explosion to his face during a past physical life. That magnitude of trauma may become embedded within the vibrational fabric of an individual's spiritual being thus creating energy distortions at that site of trauma. With the etheric field serving as a framework of energy unto which dividing cells organize the developing fetus will ultimately bear the scars of that recorded trauma. The result in this case being blindness at birth.

Perhaps the most extensive work documented in support of this phenomena comes from Dr. Ian Stevenson. He is a psychiatrist and scientific investigator who spent 30 plus years researching cases of children who were born with either birthmarks or birth defects, which are believed to be impressions from fatal injuries that were sustained during a prior physical life. These children actually remembered their previous life including the manner in which they died. The children would begin to verbalize these memories as soon as they could, usually around the age of two. A child born with missing fingers remembered being slain with swords where her hands were the first part of her body to be injured. A young boy born with a terrible malformation of his right ear and portion of his face remembered being shot in the right side of his head with a gun at close range. These children are documented as being able to recall names of family, friends, and even their killers from a prior physical life. Some, when given the opportunity, were even able to recognize them and call them by name. If still alive, grown children of the re-born person would quiz the child on certain facts that only the deceased individual would know, like the name of a wife, an occupation, or a favorite hobby.

However, Dr. Stevenson also showed that as these children aged their memories of their prior life began to fade. By the age of eight or nine years old they displayed little recollection, indicating also that there seems to be that window of time where a child's consciousness is highly attuned to realm of the spirit. The stories Dr. Stevenson collected are truly amazing. His extensive research has produced a multi-volume work and is summarized in a 248 page piece he called, *When Biology and Reincarnation Intersect*. It provides case after case of true examples of previous life trauma causing efferent influences on fetal development. Fatal injuries recorded within the fabric of the etheric field of an individual, which is carried forth in the physical body of a subsequent existence.

Indeed the arrival of new life is truly a wondrous miracle, one that can only be orchestrated by powers far greater than any physical being. Much about the creation and development of new life is out of direct control of human beings. Yet, as humans with spiritual wisdom, we can try to provide an optimal environment in which to sustain new life, if we are to serve as an integral part in which a soul arrives to our world. When we appreciate our existence with this spiritual knowledge, our roles become more defined, our options for health a little clearer, and the bestowal of imperfection made more endurable. The entrance of physical life involves so much more than egg uniting with sperm. And when things go wrong with fetal development the significance of spirit is all-encompassing. The presence and circumstances of the soul is fundamental to the gestation and birth of new life, not only for mother and child but for the universe.

CHAPTER NINE

BECOMING ACQUAINTED WITH THE BABY'S

ESSENCE BEFORE BIRTH

"We've all been waiting for you. For you. Your arrival has been marked, has been recorded on Earth, in the Universe, in the galaxies, in all of space, in all of time."

Rita Ramsey

Andrea*, a patient of mine and new mother of a baby girl, confided that she had had several encounters with her daughter's essence before she and her husband conceived this second time. Her first pregnancy had ended in her fourth month due to an incompetent cervix, and as you would imagine she and her husband were devastated. After planning to undergo a cervical cerclage, should she again conceive (a procedure where the opening of the cervix is stitched to prevent spontaneous abortion), Andrea and her husband were still somewhat hesitant in becoming pregnant because of the emotional trauma of their recent loss. But during a span of about six months, Andrea and her husband had the most magnificent experiences with their soon-to-be daughter.

Andrea and her husband considered themselves pragmatic people. They both believed in a higher being but did not strictly

127

practice any one religion. And they were uncertain about the idea of reincarnation of souls. That has since however, changed.

Andrea explained to me that over those six months after her pregnancy loss she and her husband had a string of unexplainable events occur, each involving the presence of one little girl. And it seemed as though each encounter was precipitated by Andrea or her husband expressing reluctance over again trying to conceive. Andrea described how at least five times she would be awakened from sleep by a child's voice softly calling, "Mommy, Mommy". She said the tone of voice was not alarming, but as though a child were simply calling her parent from another room. She, of course, would then get up from bed and search in the direction where the voice came from. The voice, she told me, would always seem to come from the spare bedroom, one that would become a nursery room if they were ever able to start a family. Seeing no one in the room, Andrea would look out the windows to see if perhaps she heard a child who was outdoors. Still no one. Andrea would return to bed and ask her husband if he heard anything, each time he did not.

Then something even stranger happened. One evening, before her husband arrived from work, she heard the sound of quick footsteps in her hallway. When she went to see where the sound was coming from, she was stunned at what she saw. For just a moment she saw the image of a little girl, about five years old, standing at the doorway of her spare bedroom with her arms open in the gesture of a hug. Then the image seemed to disappear with the blink of an eye. Andrea confided that the most astonishing part about the whole experience was not what she saw, but how she *felt*. She told me she did not feel fear, but instead felt a wave of love wash over her at the sight of the little girl. The entire episode left Andrea feeling dazed and terribly confused. Worried her husband may think the trauma of losing their first pregnancy was taking its emotional toll, she decided not to tell him what happened.

That is until one night her husband awoke from a dream visibly shaken. He awoke Andrea and told her he had had a vivid dream about a little girl. In his dream, this little girl appeared and told him, "Please don't give up on me. You're supposed to be my Daddy". Andrea said she froze. She asked her husband what the little girl looked like. The description was identical to that of the little girl she saw in the hallway several weeks before. Andrea then told her husband about the incident that occurred to her with the little girl. They both sat there until the wee hours of the morning, trying to make sense of all that was happening. The one thing they knew for certain was that they both emerged from their experiences with a strange sense of affection toward this apparition. And they no longer felt apprehensive of trying to conceive again. After the husband's dream, the little girl did not appear to them again. Yet both instinctively knew they would meet again.

Three months later Andrea conceived, underwent a cervical cerclage without complications, endured twelve weeks of bed rest, and gave birth to a beautiful baby girl. But as Andrea and her husband would tell you, they knew who their baby was before she was even born.

Communication with the spirit of an unborn child is not as peculiar or uncommon as one might think. I have had numerous patients tell me that they have had "encounters" with their child before their birth. It may be that a mother-to-be hears a favorite lullaby played strangely often, that a father-to-be has several dreams about the same little boy, or perhaps a soon-to-be sibling curiously receives visits from an "imaginary friend" shortly before his mother conceives. Encounters may manifest through meditation, dreams, and waking states. And, of course, the child need not be biologically connected to the family member. As I presented in the previous chapters, the uniting of souls in the physical world is not a random event limited to the rationalization of genetics, chance, or coincidence. Souls with whom you are meant to share your incarnated life will find their way to you. Whether they came from your gamete or from half-way across the Earth.

There are ways to enhance your ability of communicating with your soon-to-be child. What is required is that you tap into your natural potential to intuit. The following advice is to help you increase your intuition in general. *You do not have to be "psychic" in terms of being able to tell the future, or read people's minds, or communicate with the deceased.* For most of us that will never happen, at least during this lifetime. What is certainly attainable is a sharp and accurate sense of intuition. Intuition is the ability to become aware of something without necessarily perceiving it with our five senses. It is the understanding of the vibrational language of the soul which is often subtle and symbolic. The key elements that assist in perceiving information from the spiritual realm are: 1) the comprehension of what I have discussed in this book thus far. 2) The ability to withdraw your consciousness from the hustle and bustle and materialism of everyday life. 3) Awareness of the energy in your own body. 4) Interpreting the symbolism of dreams. 5) Asking for spiritual guidance through prayer with all of the above.

1) The comprehension of what I have discussed in this book thus far.

When we understand the *true* purpose of new life, as I have described in Part Two of this book, a whole new perspective of our existence should emerge. With that may come the ability to see the spiritual significance of all in our physical world. Information from the spiritual realm is constantly around us, but in order to perceive spiritual communication we must view life through the eyes of the soul.

2) The ability to withdraw your consciousness from the hustle and bustle and materialism of everyday life.

I have come to appreciate that this is probably one of the hardest things to do. The ability to separate ourselves from the commotion of everyday life requires that we slow down and surrender the notion of having complete control of our lives. Allow yourself to take in the beauty of a sunset, inhale the sweet smell of a child's skin when she embraces you, permit the tears to fall from your eyes when something touches your heart.

So often we are utterly caught up in managing every aspect of our lives and we fail to enjoy the journey of life. There is exquisiteness in simply being alive. Let go of the illusion of control and pause to allow the spirit in all to move us deep within. When we preoccupy ourselves on the physical we cannot see the spiritual in life all around us. There is spirit in the trees you walk by, there is spirit in the potted plant on your desk, there is spirit in the very ground you walk on. Can you slow down long enough to appreciate their radiance? If you can you are opening up yourself to intuition.

3) Awareness of the energy in your own body.

Sense the energy of your own body. What is it telling you? Does your heart feel heavy because your husband recently forgot your birthday? Does your head ache from denying to yourself that you truly hate your job? Once we sensitize and familiarize ourselves to the energies of our own soul it makes sensing outside vibrational influences much easier.

Get into the habit of monitoring your body and essence everyday in response to people, situations, and surroundings. Do certain people make you feel uncomfortable or energetically drained when they are in your presence? Were there times when you *felt* the intensity of someone staring at you before you actually caught their gaze? These are all examples of perceiving spiritual energies. But it requires the capacity to tune into the dynamics of your own energy flow, and recognize the subtle changes your body experiences in response to another spiritual dynamic.

Try this exercise. Have someone you know stand behind you. Instruct that person to position themselves about a distance of four to six inches away from your back. Close your eyes. What are you feeling? What is telling you, outside of your five senses, that someone is behind you? Is there mild tingling on your back or a subtle throbbing? Do you perceive a cool or warm sensation? Most people can discern a subtle change in their body when the energies of another spiritual being touches their own. The more in tune you are to your own essence, the more sensitive you will be to the energies of all spiritual beings.

You may also want to try flower essences (a.k.a. flower remedies) to enhance your spiritual awareness and increase the ability to tune into your unborn child. Flower essences are a type of complementary treatment used safely by many. They work by bridging the energies of body and soul. Originally discovered by English physician, Dr. Edward Bach, each flower essence was found to contain a distinct imprint or energy pattern of the specific flower. Flower essences come in tincture form, an infusion of fresh blossoms preserved in brandy and stored in a dropper bottle. They are known to deepen our contact with our spiritual selves and stimulate personal growth. Specifically, essence of the flower Forget-Me-Not can help promote consciousness of the soul bonds and karmic connections you share with this most precious being in your body.

These remedies are usually taken orally but because of its alcohol content some may be concerned about ingesting it while pregnant. Though I must point out that at the recommended dosage (two drops four times a day), the amount of alcohol ingested is scant. Nevertheless, you may want to consider bathing in the flower essence instead. Add twenty drops of Forget-Me-Not essence to a bath tub of warm water.

Stir the bath water in a figure eight motion for at least one minute to awaken its qualities. Soak in your flower essence bath for about twenty minutes. Gently pat your skin dry and take some time to absorb the subtle quality of the essence while quietly connecting to your baby.

People who have used Forget-Me-Not report gaining deeper understanding and appreciation of the soul bonds with which we unite during our lifetime. Relationships take on new meaning as our timeless connections become clearer. So soak in a bath of Forget-Me-Not and see how it can help illuminate that timeless bond with your unborn baby. You can learn more or purchase Forget-Me-Not and many other different flower essences from FES Quintessentials, (www.fesflowers.com or 800-548-0075).

4) Interpreting the symbolism of dreams.

No matter what life may have you believe, the Heavens want you to succeed in your endeavors toward spiritual progression. Spiritual guidance for helping us all on our individual journeys presents itself in many forms throughout a lifetime. It can arise in unexpected endings, beginnings, and relationships, just to name a few. But perhaps one of the most common ways in which the Heavens can assist us everyday is through the use of dreams.

Each time we enter deep sleep we have access to the spiritual realm, however, not every dream offers a clear representation of it. Because the rational mind resists the surrender of logic, dreams are often the product of reason applied to benevolent spiritual messages. The result is usually a confusing but symbolic arrangement of people, places, and situations which can be very challenging to interpret. When the mind interferes with the spiritual delivery of guidance, psychological analysis of dreams is very helpful. The field of psychology has long studied the symbolic nature of dreams and what purpose they serve in our lives. Not surprising then is the fact that these professionals conclude that dreams play a vital role in helping us lead a full and productive life, by offering us practical advice and insight. The great psychologist Carl Jung believed that when we dream we have access to intelligence outside of ourselves, a source of knowledge he called the "Collective Unconscious". I strongly advise that you get yourself a good dream dictionary, one that recognizes the spiritual power of dreams. The one I use is "The Complete Dream Dictionary" by Pamela Ball. Its accuracy in dream interpretation is bone-chilling and serves as a wonderful resource.

However, even the best dream interpretation resources cannot always decipher the very unique and individual dream experiences one may have. Sometimes the soul of an unborn child can take the form of someone else within the dream setting in a symbolic manner. I knew a woman who had an encounter with her soon-to-be son, only the image presented to her was that of her nephew who she adored. Why was the child shown to the woman as her nephew? Probably because the strong emotional bond she felt for the child in the dream made better sense to her logical mind to be for her nephew, not for an unfamiliar little boy. How can we know for certain, with all the various symbolism, that our dream experience was in fact with the essence of an unborn child? Assess the reaction of your heart to the dream. Did you feel an intense, unconditional love toward the being in the dream, even if you did not recognize him/her as someone you know or now love? Did you sense a deep maternal/paternal connection to the being, whether in the dream or upon awakening? The mind may skew the presentation of a dream, but the heart has clear, pure perception. Tune into your essence, it will tell you whether something magnificent happened during your sleep.

It is possible to have a clear dream, one that needs little or no interpretation. However, it is usually a powerful spiritual experience, one that does not occur very often. Obviously meant to impress you for a significant reason, these types of dreams can be prophetic, they can be journeys to past lifetimes, or sometimes profound encounters with spiritual beings. This type of dream is unusually vivid; you will awaken with a definite sense that the dream was different from others you have had. It was this kind of dream that introduced Andrea's husband to their unconceived daughter. A glorious straight-forward visit from a child's essence, it will undoubtedly stir your soul.

All three of my children appeared to me in my dreams before their births, however they were each shown to me as they were in life just before the demise of their physical body. My children were shown to have each perished at a very young age at the hands of an adult. In each realistic dream I viewed the events as though I were a remote spectator. I watched in horror and sorrow at how my children were treated during their short previous incarnated lives. I seemed to have shared that last lifetime with only one of them, my son Ethan. And in the dream, I was a person who had the capacity to protect him from the harm of his "then" mother, but I failed to do that. I will never forget how I awoke from that dream sobbing uncontrollably, knowing within the depths of my soul how I was indebted to the essence of my unborn child.

Dream encounters with your soon-to-be child, can manifest in subtle ways requiring interpretation or dramatic displays of spiritual happenings. If you are finding it difficult to either receive or understand your unborn child's attempt to communicate with you, ask for spiritual support; which leads me to my last point.

5) Asking for spiritual guidance through prayer with all of the above.

Lets face it, it takes a well seasoned intuitive to effortlessly undertake and achieve all that I have just mentioned. But as I have said earlier, spiritual guidance is always available and accessible. One need only ask for it and be open to it when it arrives.

But many people do not routinely pray, and in fact become uncomfortable because they are not sure how to. You can start by simply opening up a dialogue with the Higher Being you are at ease addressing. I personally address several Higher Beings when I pray, including divine Masters, Teachers, and my own spiritual Guides. However, this is a very individual choice and you must decide what brings you the most comfort when praying.

Next, find your own words. You need not recite a familiar religious prayer in order to talk to God, though some people prefer to commence praying this way. *The key element in prayer is the intent to open up communication between you and a Greater Power.* Chanting, singing, dancing, and even silence are all forms of prayer, as long as you focus your attention and receptivity on the energy of God. Pray several times a day, it can take just a minute or two. One immediate benefit of praying is that it relieves stress. Ask for spiritual guidance with sincerity, for I have found that when one asks with an open heart guidance becomes clearer.

Practice recognizing assistance by recording your dreams, noticing synchronicities and other happenings that might seem unusual or unexpected. Many times guidance is presented to us, but we either fail to perceive it or deny the message. Just before I miscarried one of my pregnancies, I dreamt I was at an airport expecting to greet someone who was about to arrive. After waiting with much anticipation, I finally saw a baby girl arrive at the gate, and I became very excited realizing she was what I was waiting for. Only she stopped at the gate and did not continue toward me. Instead, the baby girl looked at me and gestured toward a young woman next to her who resembled a cousin of my husband's named Elizabeth, who lives in Portugal. The child told me she was going to arrive at the same time as the young woman's baby. She held out her arms to me but retreated back behind the airport gate. I felt heartbroken when I awoke from that dream. Mentally I tried hard not to think much of it, refused to accept that the dream may have been foreboding. Yet, intuitively, I knew it was somewhat ominous. Days later, eleven weeks into my pregnancy, an ultrasound image confirmed the conceptus had no heartbeat.

Within a year I unexpectedly became pregnant again. Several days after confirming there was indeed a heartbeat we received word from Portugal that Elizabeth was also expecting a baby, with a due date within days of mine. I knew then that my "passenger" was indeed going to "arrive" this time. I had been shown exactly that through my dream, only I denied the message.

BOY OR GIRL?

Aside from wanting to know about the unborn child's health, traditionally one of the most pressing questions of an impending birth is, will the baby be a girl or a boy? Ask any expectant mother what question she is most asked, and she will tell you it is, "Do you want a girl or a boy?" Regardless of the answer, if you ask the same women after the birth whether they somehow knew, without the aid of diagnostics, what they were having, and chances are they will tell you, "Yes".

I have done my own informal survey of pregnant patients, family and friends. I was curious to know how many women accurately foretold the sex of their unborn child. I noted that roughly 60% - 70% of the pregnant women were able to somehow sense the sex of their baby. Most women claimed they "just knew", sometimes from the very moment they discovered they conceived. But what is it exactly that they sense? When asked for detail the majority of women described simply an awareness of either a girl quality or boy quality whenever focusing on their unborn child. Some of those who could not predict the sex explained they were unable to distinguish a particular quality, at times they sensed a boy, other times a girl. In truth they were aware of both the masculine and feminine energies in their unborn child.

I knew from the start my firstborn was a boy, and I was certain my last born was a girl. However, not I, nor any one else for that matter, was able to accurately predict the sex of my middle child. I sensed both boy and girl qualities, but slightly more girl. Everyone else, friends, family and even strangers who would approach my swollen abdomen would pronounce "that's a girl". But to everyone's surprise I gave birth to a boy. A boy who up to his present age of eleven is very gentle, sensitive, hates sports and plays a lot with girls. When he was younger he would call his video game travel bag his "purse". Indeed, when I had that memorable dream of him while I was pregnant, Ethan was a girl. Though he is one of the sweetest and most thoughtful human beings this world is graced with, I cannot help but worry if he is happy as a boy with feminine qualities. Why one would choose life as a certain gender over the other is an answer only available to that soul and his Creator.

The sex of a child brings with it a whole set of gender specific expectations like a little boy's desire to play with trucks or action figures, and a little girl's wish to care for her dolls. Boys normally have a masculine character and girls a feminine, right? But the spirit is composed of both masculine and feminine energy. It has no true gender for it transcends the carnality of human sexuality. Each soul is uniquely unisex, however it can have a propensity for particular gender characteristics. In other words, the traits we consider as being masculine such as aggression, courage, or competitiveness, can belong to the soul of an incarnated girl. As a woman, she may emerge as, say, ambitious or gutsy, and these traits may serve her well throughout her life. The ones we consider feminine like nurturing and gentleness can be part of the essence of an incarnated boy. As a man he may develop as sensitive and sympathetic, attributes which can make him a wonderful companion and father.

Between eighteen and thirty-six months a child starts to figure out what it means to be, a girl or a boy. However for many children it is not until puberty hits that they truly begin behaving like their own gender. We all know of boys who were offensively called "sissies", and girls who were called "tomboys" while growing up. Yet when they became teenagers the vast majority of them had no identity problems, largely due to the massive influence of those lovely sex hormones. But what happens when a soul's gender characteristics are exceptionally entrenched in their being, but yet they are in the body of the opposite sex? And even the onslaught of powerful hormones cannot help them assimilate to their biological assignment? I will leave that question for you to ponder. However, can you imagine a teenager's personal challenge in this situation, let alone how society judges a possible outcome?

Just another word or two about gender. Today there are couples who go to great lengths to influence Mother Nature's control over their baby's sex. This is yet another attempt at controlling nature's processes. There are now various books written by doctors that advise how to conceive a baby with the sex of your choice. Couples are trying methods like making love in certain positions and/or timing intercourse during a specific point of ovulation in hopes of manipulating what may outwardly seem as chance. Unfortunately for these couples reputable studies indicate there is no proven effectiveness of these tactics. According to researchers, when conceiving a baby gender is always a gamble, one that you must be willing to accept no matter what you are blessed with. True, but is it really the random event science purports? Perhaps the sex we are born with is yet another of God's domains which, we as carnal beings, have no business trying to control. Because God operates from a script larger than we could possibly comprehend, I am certain there is purpose in whether we experience life as a woman or a man.

And finally, even if a person still cannot perceive the essence of their soon-to-be child, despite doing as I suggested, I would advise everyone to speak to their unborn baby frequently, whether in the womb or afar. Although the child may not have knowledge of the words spoken, the message of welcoming love will certainly resound throughout her soul, and undoubtedly provide her with a blissful journey into being.

Chapter Ten

A Gentle Arrival for the New Life

"You come with a birthright, written in love and sung through all Creation in words which promise, that no matter where you're at, you're home. That no matter who you're with, you're welcome. That no matter who you are, you're loved. Welcome."

Rita Ramsey

Not much else changes your life in so many ways as having a child. Pregnancy and childbirth are life altering events for women and their involved partners. Many women enter their birthing facility as a private and reserved individual only to succumb later to the throes of labor and literally let it all hang out. Indeed, the birthing process can tell a woman a lot about herself that she previously did not know. Like the strength of her endurance, the magnificence of her body, and yes, the fact that there exists an occasion where she will not give a hoot who sees her in the most private of body positions. And I certainly say this not to put fear in the heart of any pregnant woman. Quite the contrary, I make these statements to make her aware of the power and brilliance bestowed on the birthing mother. I strongly encourage pregnant women to embrace this truly magical time, a time when their own soul allows the entrance of another into this world. To this day, I am still deeply moved by each and every birth I witness, for there is such beauty in the hope a child's spirit brings for our world and our progression. It is my firm belief that having a child, whether yours biologically or not, is not a right, but privilege.

Pregnancy and childbirth is a time when a woman should be educating herself on the many wondrous changes her body and that of her unborn baby undergoes. She and her involved partner should learn about the course of childbirth, what birthing choices are available to them, and what to expect in both a normal delivery and one that requires medical intervention. They should certainly sign up for childbirth preparation courses and tour the birthing facility before the big day approaches. There are numerous options available today that can help make your birthing experience a gloriously fulfilling one, like obtaining the support of a doula and water birthing, which can enhance peacefulness and pain control. I strongly urge expectant parents to read educational materials that emphasize the very natural process of childbirth, ones that inspire them to take an active role in their birth experience and discourages submissiveness on this most important event in their lives. I highly recommend any pregnancy and birth books written by authors Sheila Kitzinger, and Martha Sears, R.N. and her husband William Sears, M.D.. These authors are very intuitive individuals who capture the sacredness of childbirth and assist parents in realizing a truly harmonious arrival of their precious gift.

So many times I have seen couples surrender *their* experience to the authority of their well-meaning, but very occupied, physician. To my expectant readers, what you need to know is that you must work to make the birthing experience your own. No matter how caring the physician is, she has a ton of other responsibilities she must be mindful of while attending to your birth. Many of the procedures she orders are *routine* and quite possibly can be negotiated in terms of your vision for your individual birthing experience. Say for example, you prefer to not have intravenous fluids during birth because you desire to walk about unencumbered by an I.V. pole. Intravenous fluids are often routinely ordered, not so much because the birthing woman is at risk for dehydration, but to ensure easy access for medication administration via I.V. route should the need arise. Your physician may agree to only having intravenous access by the use of a saline-lock, an I.V. catheter inserted and taped to your arm but not hooked up to the tubing and bags. If the course of the pregnancy has been uncomplicated there is no reason, aside from maintaining precautionary measures, such as occasional fetal monitoring and I.V. access, why laboring couples cannot experience the birth of their child without medical intrusion.

You may also want to consider obtaining a certified midwife instead of a physician for the obstetrical care. Certified midwives are skilled and competent clinicians who advocate non-intervention in the normal processes of pregnancy and childbirth. These caring practitioners encourage active participation of their patients and their families as well as providing education, emotional, and social support throughout the childbearing experience. Always working with a physician as a back up measure in the event of an obstetrical emergency, the certified midwife is a safe, highly satisfying alternative to an M.D. for normal pregnancies.

Another lovely option for the birthing woman is the service of a labor doula. A labor doula is a certified professional labor assistant who supports the mother throughout the birth of her child. A doula takes care of the mother's emotional needs, provides guidance, and suggests techniques to enhance labor progress. Essentially, she mothers the mother. She is the woman's advocate and helps her partner with his important role during the baby's birth. Employing a doula can dramatically reduce the chances of the birthing mother having a cesarean section and decreases length of labor, the need for pain medications, and the use of other medical interventions. To find a certified doula, you may go to www.DONA.org and use their directory or ask a midwifery practice to recommend one.

Quite honestly, I can go on and on about how to make the birthing experience one to truly savor, but I must stop here or risk digression. The important point is that I strongly advise you and your involved partner to thoroughly prepare yourselves for the impending birth, educate yourselves on what to expect, even the particulars of an undesirable outcome. The goal is to empower yourself with education, to replace fear and anxiety with understanding and confidence. I ask that you leave nothing to surprise you. Have a birthing plan, but also have some understanding of what events are occurring if something goes wrong. This will help you to accept a modification in your birth plan should you require unexpected medical intervention.

I once had a patient who, because she was prepared for and envisioned only a normal vaginal birth, became extremely upset after her son was delivered via emergency cesarean section. So disappointed was she that within four months of her son's birth she became pregnant again. Only her motivation for having another child so soon was not because it was part of her family plan; it was because she could not accept the circumstances of her son's cesarean birth and absolutely felt driven not to "fail" again. Unfortunately, in her emotional distress, she neglected to learn about her chances of having the birth she so desperately required. Because the uterine incision of her cesarean section was only a year old, her obstetrician refused to deliver her next child vaginally for fear her uterus might rupture under the force of labor contractions and maternal pushing. As one would expect, the woman was devastated. However, before her second child was born, she came to terms with her outcomes with the help of counseling, and welcomed her new child's healthy arrival.

Keep in mind also, that no matter how much you prepare yourselves, no matter which top practitioner you obtain, and regardless of where you choose to safely have your baby, that sometimes things happen that are not within yours, or anyone else's control. Always remember that the Heavens influence life in a manner that is all-encompassing and that unfortunate events, though incomprehensible at the time, ultimately have some shred of purpose. And that purpose may even have nothing to do with you. What *is* in your power is the readiness of your mind, body, and soul for the birth of your baby. Education, self-care, intuition, and the graceful influence of prayer is in your control, carry out each to the best of your ability. I encourage you also to take advantage of the wonderfully therapeutic services that are now available for pregnant women, such as prenatal massage and yoga, for even more serenity during this magical time.

So now you have become at ease with what to anticipate during your child's arrival, and feel confident in your ability to advocate for safe, personal birth choices. Now allow the inflow of intuition. Slow down and sense the gradual coming of your baby's essence to your womb. Your baby is on a celebrated journey into being, her hopes and aspirations for this lifetime are well anticipated between herself and the Powers who guided her here. Recall that the union of body and soul in the womb is a slow and gentle process. The etheric layer of your baby's essence was present since implantation occurred six to ten days after conception. However, it is the higher and finer energies of the child's essence that gradually descends upon its developing physical body; that when completed, the baby is ready to safely be born. Heighten your awareness, and you just may sense exactly when her essence has arrived.

I talked briefly about the nesting urge in Chapter 7 and how it seems that this is when most women (and other females in the animal kingdom) may in fact be sensing the entrance of their baby's complete essence within their own being. It appears almost logical when one considers the very characteristics of the nesting urge. A sudden increase in physical energy is a common occurrence for women experiencing the nesting urge. When the essence of the baby completes his journey to body this adds to the spiritual energy dynamic of his mother. The physical body of the mother reasonably responds to the increase in her own vibratory flow by becoming more active. However, her soul knows what has occurred. And while her rational mind cannot explain the use of her physical energy toward preparing her environment for the impending arrival of her baby, her guiding higher awareness knows exactly what it is doing.

Another telltale sign of nesting urge is a pregnant woman's inexplicable desire to stay in or close to home with only familiar people around her. The obvious message here from baby's essence to mom's is, "I have arrived and will be born soon, so don't venture off too far."

The nesting urge is most often explained in the textbooks as Mother Nature's way of helping ensure that the mother's environment is safe and ready for when baby arrives. Yet I believe this explanation takes away from the true loveliness of what it really is. For in its purest form, nesting urge *is* demonstrable communication between the souls of mother and baby; regard and honor this precious awareness as such. Over 70% of pregnant women experience this interaction with their unborn baby within weeks or days before birth. Even if you were unable to perceive your baby prior to her nearing birthday do not dishearten, chances are you will sense the completion of her journey by recognizing your urge to nest.

As your due date approaches, conversations with and focused thought on your baby should now include his having a safe arrival. *Remember, although the child does not know language yet he can certainly perceive the exquisite vibrations of love and the intent of your message at any point during your pregnancy.* Describe to your baby what you anticipate your day to be like. Have fun and playfully tell him that if he plans to arrive today a good time would be after his dad comes from work, not when you are at the mall and two hours away from home because it also happens to be rush hour. This is especially important if he is not your first baby and you have a history of having fast labors (less than 6 hours). Always keep in mind, that the *baby* initiates his birth. So if your body responds easily to your baby's triggers of beginning the birthing process, go ahead and exercise some parental guidance by trying to coax your baby's timely arrival.

I have quick labors. My first child took five hours to be born and my second child burst into our world a mere two hours after my first contraction. The two hours were barely enough time to page my midwife, call my in-laws to stay with my then three year old son, get dressed, and get to the hospital, which fortunately was only 20 minutes away from home. Thank the Heavens all of this was accomplished in just about an hour. By the time I got to the hospital I was five centimeters dilated and bombarded with the powerful contractions of active stage labor. A little over an hour later, my second son was born.

When I learned I was pregnant with my daughter I grew concerned over my future birthing event. We had since moved further away from the hospital, approximately 45 minutes away from where we lived, and my husband was working six days a week, 12 hour days at a job site an hour away from home (he owns a construction business). Anticipating an even quicker labor than my second, I literally prepared myself for the possibility of either having my baby delivered en route to the hospital by EMS, or birthing our baby by myself at home. But I also talked to my unborn daughter everyday, lovingly expressing my concern. The intent of my prayer to her and God at that point was not to have an idealistic birthing experience, but instead to ensure that she enter our world unharmed through the yielding nature of my own womb. I asked that she somehow give me sufficient warning of her impending arrival, just enough time so that I might give her the tenderly safe welcome she so deserved.

The events which led up to my daughter's birth still deeply move me, as she gave me subtle signs of her coming over the course of forty-eight hours. First, I had painful but irregular contractions throughout the early morning two days before her birth, which caused a "false alarm" trip to the hospital. Then I passed a bloody show twenty-four hours before her birth, an occurrence which is common with pregnant women about to give birth, but one I had never experienced. Next, the morning of the day she was born, I felt strange pulling sensations across my back and passed more bloody show just before my husband awoke to leave for work that day. Lastly, I just *knew* she would come that day. My husband and I drove to my midwife's office early that morning, and I was found to be four centimeters dilated, my cervix was completely thinned out, and our baby was totally engaged in my pelvis, yet oddly I had no significant uterine contractions. It was as if our baby was holding out as long as she possibly could without fully beginning her birth. My midwife sent us immediately to the nearby hospital where she ruptured my bag of water (amniotomy), which was simply to start my uterus contracting. With the process of birth well underway (and well guided), my daughter was safely born only two and half hours after we entered the hospital. For me it was a truly humbling experience in loving, spiritual communication.

Exercises to Enhance Physical Response to Baby's Birth Signals

As short labors usually occur because of the mother's body responding easily to her baby's triggers, so does the opposite rationale exist for strenuous labors. Long and hard labors usually have to do with an unintentional lack of "vibrational" communication between the mother's body and the baby's cues to be born. This may be caused by several different factors, including fear, anxiety, tension, and pain. And while the mind-body goal of childbirth preparation is to reduce these factors, a greater maternal physical response can be achieved by preparing her spiritual energies as well.

From the 38th week of gestation and on, you may begin performing several simple "energy" exercises which work to clear stagnant energy about the areas of the cervix and uterus. DO NOT perform these exercises any earlier than the 38th week of gestation. They will not cause premature labor, but you certainly do not want your body to become overly sensitive to any possible uterine activity such as that which occurs with Braxton Hicks contractions, nipple stimulation, and even sexual orgasm.

You can begin the exercises by relaxing your mind and body through deep breathing exercises and focused thought. I find that many people have "forgotten" how to effectively take deep breaths, the kind that expands the lungs to its greatest capacity, correctly known as diaphragmatic breathing. In order to get the maximum amount of air in your lungs, the diaphragm, which is a horizontal band of muscle that lies between the chest and the abdominal cavities, must pull downward. This action makes the belly rise and expands the lowest parts of the lungs to bring air to these areas often neglected when we breathe shallowly. Tension, worry, and other anxieties frequently produce what is called "shoulder" or "chest" breathing, which is respiration that only uses a limited amount of muscles. This type of breathing is a learned behavior. As carefree children we automatically breathe correctly. And when we retire from our day's worries and stresses we once again breathe properly during our time of sleep. Tonight, just before you fall asleep notice the way your abdomen, not your shoulders or chest, rise as you inhale deeply.

Deep breathing exercises can be a bit challenging when your uterus is pushing up against the bottom of your lungs. However, try your best by sitting in a comfortable chair, preferably one that reclines so the weight of your uterus is not pushed up against your ribcage by your thighs. While in a reclining position, place your hands on the bottom curve of your belly. Start breathing slowly as comfortable as you can, in through your nostrils and out through your relaxed mouth. Watch your hands and notice how they rise with each inhalation, and fall with every exhalation.

Now close your eyes and focus on the energies of your uterus. Pretend in your mind that your baby is ready to enter our world after completely uniting with her physical body in your womb. She sends out her cues to signal your body's energy to make her arrival possible by rousing your first, second, and third chakras. Visualize how your body would honor her signals. Picture your uterus nudging her, gently pushing her into our world with every squeeze of muscle contraction. Then focus on your cervix, the neck of your uterus, which looks like a miniature donut lying between your uterus and vagina. (During childbirth, uterine contractions also work to pull back the opening of the dense cervix away from the entrance to the vaginal or birth canal. The increasing size of the cervical opening is measured in centimeters, ten centimeters being fully dilated and ready to start pushing.) "See" your cervix thin out and melt away with every squeeze your uterus makes, creating an open path for your baby's journey into the physical world.

Lastly, move the energy of your solar plexus, sacral, and root chakras with your hands. Rub your hands together for a few seconds to invigorate their vibrations. Lay one of your hands within one to three inches from your skin and at the space between your navel and breastbone. Start moving your hand in a clockwise circular motion for approximately thirty seconds. Next, move your hand down to the space just below your navel and do the same thing for another thirty seconds. Do not be surprised if you feel your baby begin to squirm as he will sense the energy of your hands.

Finally, move your hand to your perineum, (or as close as you can get to it) and circle it again in a clockwise fashion. While you are moving these energies visualize a fleshy pink whorl slowly spinning in a spiral motion. With every rotation see the center of the whorl open and expand, gradually transforming it into a thin ring about four inches wide. Again perform this energy exercise for a duration of no more than 30 seconds. All exercises may be done twice a day.

If however, your labor has started (as evidenced by consistent contractions lasting over 40 seconds long and/or waters breaking) but then stalls in terms of no increase and intensification of contractions or cervical dilation, you may increase the time and frequency of these energy exercises. Especially perform them if you are at a birthing facility and hear your practitioner say that your labor is "failing to progress". At that point do them as long as you feel comfortable, although you may get a few curious stares when rotating your hand above your perineum, particularly from the male species.

A Warm and Tender Welcome

Heavens willing, your labor is surely underway and soon your baby's journey into the physical world will be complete. But there is so much harshness she will encounter starting the moment she enters our world. Within the traditional physician attended/hospital birth setting the baby's entrance may be even more jarring. No, I am not bashing physicians or hospital births; all three of my children were born in a hospital as I have mentioned before. And most physicians simply get too caught up the science of the physical body which interferes with their ability to see the needs of the spirit. As medical experts they are compelled to *control* the process of birth and are not very concerned with providing a harmonious welcome for their "delivery".

The process of birth is a phenomenal event for the incoming soul, one that need not be more harrowing than it already is. Make no mistake about it, newborn babies can perceive discomfort and pain, which are new and shocking sensations to them. Being a maternal/child health nurse working in a hospital has provided me with the experience of seeing what a newborn baby routinely goes through from his birth up to his discharge. And it is not entirely pleasant, especially for the very fragile souls who have journeyed to physicality. Now I could sit here and list all the distressing things your baby may encounter during her birth and shortly thereafter, but that may only serve to preoccupy you, and that is certainly not my intent. Instead, I will make suggestions on how to plan for an optimally nurturing experience for your baby's grand entrance, regardless of the circumstances.

First I want you to know that during the birthing process the incoming soul must adjust to an onslaught of new sensations. She will now feel the weight of her once weightless body. Instead of perfectly harmonic sound she will hear harsh tones. And where they once saw only beauty her eyes will now see a barrage of insensitive things like glaring lights and unsympathetic faces. And from an existence where physical pain and discomfort were absent she will now endure with dreadful surprise, which she will experience within the first few moments after her birth. From the pressure of suctioning her nose and mouth to the sharp pain of her first injection (vitamin K), her welcome can certainly seem unkind.

Next, I would like to introduce a concept that you will be hearing throughout the rest of this book, and that is the child's strong dependence on spiritual bonding. The energy dynamics of the newly incarnated soul is chaotic and disorganized which is an uncomfortable sensation. This discomfort can be manifested as fussiness, or to an extreme, colic (more on this subject in Chapter 11). Just imagine. Your discarnate spirit is expansive, unrestrained, graceful, and fluid; the energy of your soul flows effortlessly smooth, unencumbered by the physical form of the human body. Your soul's gradual journey to the physical body while in utero was a deliberate process for this reason. Once born, the soul's adjustment to its physical body may take as many as ten years. The most fundamental way the child can organize his chaotic energy patterns is to be surrounded within the organized energies of another, preferably the familiar vibrations of the mother. Physically embracing a child envelopes them in your spiritual aura. Depending on your particular vibratory essence this can either soothe the child or cause further discomfort. I will provide more detail in the next chapter. For now it is important you understand the newborn's challenges and his need for spiritual bonding through physical closeness.

That said, if you honor the needs of your baby's essence during his first few days of life his adaptation to the physical world should be easier on him. Ask your practitioner if she will allow immediate physical contact with your baby after birth. If this is impossible, as when undergoing a cesarean section, request that your partner be able to embrace your newborn shortly after his birth. Too often we as new parents permit hospital staff to unjustifiably create separateness between ourselves and our healthy baby by whisking him away to a nursery moments after his birth. This is wrong, and goes against a very basic instinct of bonding with your baby soon after he is born. If your baby requires medical care, and once you are physically able, ask to participate in his care. **Above all else, ensure that your baby be touched and embraced frequently, if at all possible.** Numerous studies have proven the healing effects of touch on babies and children. They thrive from frequent physical contact achieving quicker recovery times with improved immune systems, enhanced growth, and reduced stress hormones, just to name a few benefits. *Spiritual bonding is the foundation of this consequence.* Children lose precious life energy while attempting to organize their own patterns, energy which can be well spent on regeneration, healing, and growth. Blanketing your child in your own loving vibratory radiance helps his energy to find some order, order that soothes his soul and body.

If you and your baby are physically able, ask that she room-in with you. There may be both full and modified rooming-in options available at your birthing facility. Modified rooming-in is when your baby is with you the majority of the day, but is brought back to the nursery several times during the day and all night. Your baby will be brought to you, if you choose, every 3-4 hours during the night for feedings. This option may be suitable for the mother who is experiencing medical problems and cannot respond to or care for her baby as necessary in the immediate postpartum period. However, every effort should be made to change to full rooming-in as soon as mother is feeling able to safely care for her own baby. As you read on you will discover why. And I will say this, although I suffered from a painful joint condition known as pubis symphasis diastasis, (separation of the pelvic bones) I made sure my baby was with me throughout our hospital stay despite my pain. Am I seeking martyrdom? Heck no, I simply refused to allow my baby's first days of physical life to be either alone in a hospital bassinette, or in the arms of someone who did not cherish her. I now know too much about her journey into being to permit that.

Full rooming-in means baby is with you day and night. Baby goes back to the nursery only for medical exams or procedures, and when you request that he return when you want to shower or get some rest. Having your baby with you for as much time as possible after his birth is most beneficial for both you and baby. In addition to helping your baby's energies find some order, close contact with him will increase your natural intuition and responsiveness to him. The ability to sense what your baby is feeling, and thus knowing what he needs creates a natural easiness in parenting.

Do not be afraid or intimidated by your new role as a mother (or father), trust your own spirit to sense what your baby needs and wants. It is entirely possible to intuit what your baby's soul is experiencing as he adapts to his new form in the physical world. Begin as soon as you can after your baby's birth. While you are alone with your baby (try starting in the room of your birthing facility), close your eyes and temporarily forget every child rearing advice you received from *anyone,* including family members, physicians, parenting experts, etc.. Look, listen, and feel your baby; then sense the radiance of his energy. What does it feel like when he is calm? Try to sense the difference in his vibratory essence when he is calm/alert and calm/sleepy. What about when he begins to cry? What does the intensity of his chaotic energy flow telling you? Do you sense the sharpness of pain, or the dullness of discomfort? The vast majority of times when a healthy newborn baby cries it is because he is expressing the discomfort of his frenzied spirit as it adapts to the physical body. Obey your own soul's natural instinct to embrace your child and notice the change in his essence when you hold him close to your heart. A child's cries are designed to evoke a physical response from you, however it is your baby's last resort of communication. In time, by familiarizing yourself to your baby's unique spiritual dynamics you will be able to intuit what your baby needs or wants *before* he has to cry. Many parents who are intuitively connected to their children can even sense when their baby is getting ill, before symptoms arise.

A Few Words About Infant Pain

I promised I would not detail the potentially uncomfortable encounters your baby may experience while in the care of well-meaning medical professionals. However, I do want to arm you with the information you need to advocate for the optimum pain management your baby can have during any medical procedures.

In light of the extremely vulnerable manner in which our infants arrive, it is my strong belief that unmanaged infant pain results in a lasting "imprint" on the closest spiritual layer of their physical being, the etheric layer. Recall that when we experience bodily injury this network of energy aids in the regeneration of damaged cells needed to heal. These activities of harm and repair are recorded in the etheric layer, an event we are not consciously aware of. Therefore, although an infant would not remember having physical pain this layer can become "scarred" or "distorted" with the traumatizing impression of pain endured long ago. Consequently, what may result is a child who will become quite sensitive to physical discomfort in later years. Not because their brain can recollect having pain, but their whole body of spiritual energy can.

As early as the year 2000 almost all routine procedures preformed on infants were done without pain control. From heel sticks to circumcision, *nothing* was given to prepare our children for the pain they were about to face. The common idea was that babies did not feel pain. This being the assumption because babies, of course, could not at the time verbalize the pain, nor could they recall it from memory as an older child.

But thankfully more and more research conducted on infant pain is supporting what I and many others have believed all along. And the medical community has started changing their practices. Recent studies have proven that infants undergoing a painful procedure without adequate pain control have significant physiologic changes. Stress hormones soar, the baby's heart rate and blood pressure increases, his breathing pattern changes. And intriguingly, these same studies show that when infant pain is not adequately addressed it may render the child *hypersensitive to pain* in later years. Because of these recent findings medical practitioners are now treating pain management for children very differently. Many are now routinely providing pain control and ensuring our children do not endure distress unnecessarily.

So what are some of the things you can do to ensure adequate pain management for your child? For starters, during the times when you or your partner are present for a procedure lovingly hold your child and speak to her reassuringly. Even better, have your baby breastfeed. The rationale remaining the same… children in stressful situations are helped by being embraced by the subtle energies of a loving, caring individual, preferably a parent. Breastfeeding adds two benefits. First, it has long been known that sucking physiologically provides comfort for a baby, thus the popular use of pacifiers. And second, breastfeeding stimulates the vibratory essence of the heart chakra effectively bathing the child in intense, radiant energy.

There are analgesics, topical anesthetics, and natural remedies which have been proven safe and effective in dulling the physical perception of pain. *Many children as early as infancy can be given acetaminophen about thirty minutes before a procedure to help alleviate pain experienced during and afterwards. As for topical anesthetics there are several safe agents available such as lidocaine and benzocaine which act to numb the area to be treated. These can be especially effective for immunizations and any procedures involving trauma to the skin.

(**Always discuss the appropriateness and safety of any treatment with your child's medical practitioner before taking any advice from this book. There are numerous conditions that may prevent the use of any of the above suggestions.*)

But perhaps the simplest of pain control methods for children involves something just about all of us love to occasionally indulge in - sugar. Sucrose has been found to actually block the ability to sense pain by stimulating the opioid pathways in the brain. The same region where the pleasurable effects of narcotic drugs like morphine influence. Sucrose is safe and can even be used in pre-term babies. Pain relief can be as easy as giving a child sugared water or a pacifier dipped in sugar during a procedure.

The spirit's entrance to the physical world is rarely without some level of distress. We should make every effort to usher our children in with as much beauty and comfort as humanly possible. Prompt bonding, both physical and spiritual, and adequate pain management can only ease the transition from spirit to human body.

Following the methods suggested for the gentle arrival of new life will help to initiate intuitive responsiveness with your child, and assist in starting a relationship enhanced by knowing your child's unique *soul*. Books on childcare and parenting will help guide you in terms of what to anticipate as your child grows, like when to expect developmental milestones or how to discern illness. But only you can tap into the ability to truly sense the inner being of your child, and respond to her as no advice book can. Trust that you have this capacity, and in doing so you will aid in nurturing her soul as well as her mind and body.

Before moving on to the next chapter, I would like to share a story with you about the first time I encountered intuitive parenting. While providing nursing care for postpartum moms and their babies I met a patient who displayed remarkable ease in her new role as a mother. She requested full rooming-in with her newborn son, and each time I made my rounds to her room to provide teaching on newborn care she politely declined my offer. With the exception of showing her umbilical cord care she was basically on her own.

I automatically assumed she was a veteran mom, perhaps having three or more children by the way she appeared so confident in parenting her newborn. You can imagine my surprise and intrigue when she told me this was her first child.

Each time I entered my patient's room I saw her baby nestled in her arms, at times effortlessly nursing, other times simply cuddling. What especially stood out in my mind was how little I heard her son cry. In fact, the only time I heard him cry was when I returned him to the nursery because his mother wanted to shower. My nursing colleagues took notice too, dumbstruck at how mothering came so natural to her, when we all expect to teach our new mothers how to feed, burp, diaper, handle, and otherwise care for their infant. On the day she and her son left the hospital, as I was giving her discharge instructions, I was in awe of the glowing interaction between this mother and her baby. The connection was almost palpable and I clearly had to know what was her secret for such a magical bonding with her baby. When I asked, her response was simple and straightforward. She said she read everything she needed about pregnancy, childbirth, and breastfeeding to ensure she had these "mechanics" down pat. "The rest", she told me, "was simply a matter of getting to *really* know my baby, which is something no one can do better than me." That, readers, is the heart of intuitive nurturing.

CHAPTER ELEVEN

THE CHILD'S DEPENDENCE ON SPIRITUAL BONDS

"The life I touch for good or ill will touch another life, and that in turn another, until who knows where the trembling stops or in what far place my touch will be felt."

Frederick Buechner

On October of 1995, when a set of premature twins were born, one of the two was sicker, weaker, and weighed less than her sister. After a month in the neonatal intensive care unit the weaker sister was losing her fight for life. Her breathing was becoming more labored and heart rate was poor; doctors had done all they could. In mid-November the sicker twin dramatically worsened. Her blood oxygen saturation plummeted and she began to turn blue. The nurse on staff caring for the twins, Gayle Kasparian, desperately sought a way to help her tiny patient. Remembering something she heard about the benefits of putting twins in the same bed she quickly placed the stronger, healthier twin in the same incubator as her weaker sister. Immediately the sicker infant snuggled up her stronger sister and to the amazement of everyone present she *instantly* improved the moment she and her sibling touched. She stopped crying, her vital signs stabilized, and her skin color returned to normal. Just over a month later the twins came home, both considered to be very healthy. The nation came to know of these little twins when a beautiful picture of them was published in Life Magazine and Reader's Digest. The snapshot was of them lying together in a bassinette with the stronger sibling's arm protectively draped over her sister. The picture, originally taken by an employee of the Worchester Telegram & Gazette, became famous and was known as "The Rescuing Hug". Many hospitals nationwide have now adopted the practice of "co-bedding" twins or other multiples. Though they are not sure how or why, the evidence is significant that this simple contact can dramatically reduce the physical and emotional signs of stress in hospitalized babies.

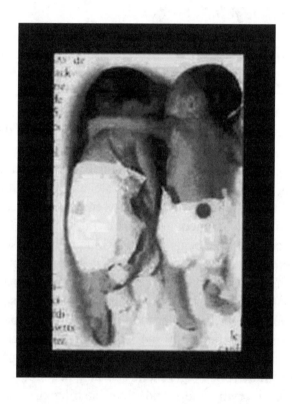

In 1983 when Columbian neurologists Edgar Rey and Hector Martinez began studying the effects of placing a premature infant on a parent's bare chest the results were equally amazing. Specifically, the doctors would put a diaper clad premature infant in an upright position tummy to tummy with mom or dad. The baby's head would be turned so that the ear is above the parent's heart. What they found was that the mortality rate of premature babies in Bogotá, where the study was taking place, fell from 70% to 30%.

Fast forward to 1997. A study done by Patricia Messmer found that when babies are placed on a parent's chest, in the same fashion as above, their sleep time is considerably increased. Many infants have trouble transitioning from one sleep state to the other because of their disorganized and immature physiology; in other words because their inner workings do not function as smooth as an older child's does. What ensues is fussiness and for some babies excess crying. In fact many researchers believe that an infant's immature physiology and subsequent inability to transition from one sleep state to the other is a major cause of colic (more on the subject of colic in the next chapter). Kangaroo Care, as this practice has aptly been termed, when performed in a quiet, low light environment will help any baby, premature or full term, with sleep transition and has proven to significantly reduce crying.

In 1998, Susan Ludington, professor of maternal/child health nursing at the University of Maryland at Baltimore, found that while babies were on their parent's chest there was a four-fold decrease in apnea (a brief pause in the infant's breathing). And mechanically ventilated babies were able to better tolerate transfer and position changes without increased oxygen requirements. And earlier in 1990 the same researcher concluded that babies placed in the Kangaroo Care position with their mother showed thermal synchrony. In other words, when the baby got cold, the mother's temperature would increase to warm up her baby. The same occurred when the baby was warm, the mother's temperature would cool her down. Even when given the verbal cue of "your baby looks warm to me" the mother's temperature would decrease within minutes to compensate.

In a study published in 1997, Holly Richardson concluded that babies gained more weight faster when they were placed in the Kangaroo Care position with their parent. When left alone on a warming table babies cried more, expended more energy, and slept less. Those who had the close physical contact would immediately be calmed and fall into a deep sleep, therefore conserving their energy and enhancing their weight gain and growth. Holly Richardson's study showed that babies who have been "Kangarooed" can have as much as a 50% shorter hospital stay than those who have not been.

To sum it up, babies both premature and full-term, can thrive from the steadier heart rates, better breathing, faster growth, improved sleep, and of course, greater contentment from simple physical contact with another loving human being, big or small. Parents who have practiced placing their child on their body for a period of time claim they experience a deep bonding and attachment to their child. They say things like they feel strongly "connected", and that there is a profound "knowing" of their child.

Let us extend that concept as the child grows. It is a well known fact that good things happen to babies who are placed in an infant carrier and "worn" by their loving caretaker. It can reduce crying and fussiness by 43% during the day and by 51% at night. It promotes energy conservation and helps to regulate baby's physiology. In other words, it too helps baby's breathing, heart rate, digestion, and temperature function better and smoother. And it enhances parent/infant attachment. Those who share this intimacy with their child also claim to have a deep and knowing bond with them. This knowing promotes a responsiveness to their child like nothing else. Parents say they can often anticipate or sense what their child needs before the child makes it obvious by fussing or crying.

Now what about bedtime? Can this kind of close physical contact work its magic on babies throughout the night, thus helping not only baby sleep but her parents as well? Overwhelming evidence says, yes. Co-bedding, as the practice of sleeping with your baby is termed, offers the same and more exquisite benefits of close contact during the day. Safely sleeping with your baby not only helps to regulate her physiology, promote deep attachments, and reduce crying as the other forms of physical contact do, but also seems to reduce the risk of her dying from sudden infant death syndrome (SIDS). Though researchers do not know for sure what causes SIDS, it seems the most reasonable explanation in most babies lies in their less organized physiological control mechanisms. Meaning their body's ability to function and adjust normally to changes. Several studies of high risk infants and babies who passed away of SIDS showed that their heart-rates were higher and less adaptable to changes. This is most likely to be caused by immature systems in the body, primarily the neurological and respiratory systems. Once again we see that babies arrive to our physical world in quite a vulnerable state.

WHAT ANTHROPOLOGISTS SAY...

Anthropologists who have studied human development comparatively with other mammals theorize that humans seem to be born about one year "too early". In contrast to many mammals which at birth have their brain size at about 80% of adult size, the human infant's brain is about 25% of that of an adult. Human children do not reach 80% of adult brain size until they are about 1 year old. During that one year of development postpartum we as caretakers of our young must provide the correct "habitat" or place designed to help the

165

infant cope with its immaturity. An optimal habitat, according to anthropological evidence, can be provided through what is termed as "carry care". Carry care is comprised of almost continuous carrying of the infant including co-sleeping of mother and infant, immediate nurturing response, carrying of the infant either in the arms or with a carrier device, frequent and continuous feeding, and breastfeeding for a period of two years or more. Anthropologists point out that it is only in Western society where parents have evolved away from "carry care" to one of "cache care" where the infant is left alone lying still, feeding are scheduled, and expected to sleep apart from their mother.

Furthermore, research indicates that when the attachment process of "carry care" is disturbed, meaning mother and newborn become separated for a time, the infant begins what is termed "protest-despair behavior". The protest response involves withdrawal, distress cries and other behaviors that indicate she is in the wrong "habitat". If separation continues, stress hormones rise, body temperature drops, heart rate slows and/or becomes irregular, physical growth slows, immune system is suppressed, and healthy sleep patterns are disturbed. Once the infant is reunited with its "correct habitat" (brought together with mother), body systems are restored and stress hormones reduce.

Now if close physical contact with baby proves to support her physiological and emotional well being it can only make sense that this closeness can provide some protection from the risk of, not only SIDS, but other potentially harmful disorders of the body. Indeed we can understand the logic involved. In fact there have been studies suggesting that the benefits of close and loving physical contact with baby extend far beyond those early childhood years. Children who were frequently carried were less likely to develop unhealthy addictions such as alcoholism, drug addiction, over-eating, and compulsive spending. I am certain proof of far more benefits is forthcoming. It is just a matter of time when the connections are made by science.

Until then I would like to present to you one powerful yet mystical facet of sharing loving intimacy with your child that protects her delicate state. It is afferent influence of the spirit as I have detailed in Chapter 3. We have heard what the researchers have uncovered, now let us consider the power of that which cannot be readily seen in the physical body. For it is there where we will see the fundamentals of *why* close physical contact can help babies so very much.

THE MEDICINAL POWER OF LOVING CONTACT

Benjamin, who was Ann's second child, was born three weeks premature. Because he was born weighing six pounds and showed no signs of physical disability he was allowed to room-in with Ann during her hospital stay. Benjamin nursed well often and Ann kept him in her arms for the majority of the day. Benjamin seemed healthy and content.

When Ann's pediatrician arrived early the day after Benjamin was born to examine him she gently took him from his mother's arms to bring him to the nursery. Immediately Benjamin began howling, in fact Ann was able to hear her son's cries from her hospital room down the hall. Ann smiled to herself thinking how Benjamin seems to already be a "momma's boy". Then suddenly Benjamin's cries stopped. It was not until Ann saw a few pediatric residents run by her room toward the nursery that she began to panic, thinking something tragic must have happened to Benjamin. When she rushed to the nursery she saw a half dozen doctors and nurses, including her pediatrician, circled around her beautiful son Benjamin who now had a tiny oxygen mask on his face. A kind nurse headed her off at the entrance of the nursery to inform her that Benjamin had an episode of apnea, a period of time where he stopped breathing. The nurse reassured Ann that Benjamin was okay now that he was again breathing normally, but that he would have to be transferred to the neonatal intensive care unit for close monitoring. Ann was both confused and devastated. How could something so wrong be happening to her baby who had just seemed so healthy and content in her arms? Ann's pediatrician later explained that Benjamin was apparently born with some immaturity of the neurological and respiratory systems, therefore putting him at risk for potentially dangerous episodes of apnea.

While in NICU, Benjamin suffered two more episodes of apnea. Ann could not help but notice that both episodes occurred just minutes after she returned him to his isolette, where he lay alone after having intimate contact with his mother nursing and cuddling. She felt silly bringing up this little seeming coincidence thinking how doctors must know if there was any logical connection.

Once he was medically stable to go home, Benjamin's pediatrician explained to Ann and her husband that he was now at increased risk for SIDS, and that they should monitor Benjamin's breathing throughout the night while he slept in his own crib. This deeply disappointed Ann because she wanted Benjamin to sleep beside her and her husband as their older child had done for the first three years of her life. But, of course, they followed the doctor's advice and rigged a monitoring device in a crib for Benjamin. Only instead of relief and peace of mind, came panic and anxiety each night because of the many times the alarm would sound; most every time in error. Not to mention how Benjamin would cry constantly when left alone in his crib. Finally after several weeks, because of sheer exhaustion and simple yielding to her own instincts, Ann removed the monitoring device from Benjamin, brought him into her bed, and never returned him.

Not once did Ann witness him stop breathing while he lay next to her as she spent many hours during those first nights simply watching her son sleep. Beside his mother Benjamin nursed often, slept calm and content, and absolutely thrived. At the slightest change in Benjamin, either shown physically or perceived, Ann would instinctively awaken if asleep and stroke his body. Benjamin would respond by immediately relaxing and either falling back to sleep or nuzzling up to his mother's breast, feeding, and drifting off again. Soon the two seemed to be in sync with one another, awakening within seconds of each other with Ann most of the time being the first. It became as if Ann intuitively sensed when Benjamin needed to arouse.

During Benjamin's fourth month check-up his pediatrician praised his development and signs of perfect health. Yet Ann did not disclose her night-time practices with Benjamin for fear that the doctor would admonish her, and think her foolish for believing that co-sleeping had something to do with his recovery. But Ann is totally convinced that her constant close contact with Benjamin is what helped his body gain the strength needed to function properly. She did not understand exactly how or why, but she did know that whenever Benjamin was close to her he was calm, nursed well, and seemed to function better physically, mentally, and emotionally. Ann knew intuitively that her son was thriving, and that was all the evidence she needed. Now at age ten Benjamin is a healthy and active fifth grader.

Researchers too do not know for certain just how close physical contact helps babies so much. Many theorize that this kind of contact promotes an exchange of sensory stimuli such as movement, touch, vision, smell, temperature, and carbon dioxide which stimulates respiration. Yes, that does make a lot of sense. But it does not answer the emotional and behavioral benefits like dramatically less fussing, crying, disorganized movements, and more time spent in calm quiet-alert states. Others add that close contact with your infant renders you better able to pick-up on subtle changes. Definitely logical. But some go so far as to admit that this intimate contact may produce an "intuitive" type of response from the parent. *Intuitive*... Let us explore that and why close contact stimulates not only the physical systems within of our babies but touches the very core of their being. And as such can have a profound impact on their physical, mental, and emotional well-being.

The Vibrational Element

In Chapter 3, I detailed what made children so different in terms of their unstable energy flow and sensitivity to extraneous spiritual energies. Indeed, they are unique in that they are exceptionally vulnerable yet naturally intuitive. Recall how the souls of babies, being newly incarnated with limited means of communication, receive their information about other beings by perceiving the person's spiritual energy. In a way this sensitivity is a survival tactic offering the child a means of perceiving with accuracy that which can give him sustenance, his mother. This is one of the reasons why a baby will be immediately calmed in the arms of his mother. The spiritual essences of most babies and some older children, with their unorganized energies, can easily be affected by the subtle energies of others. Again this is why some infants will cry in the arms of certain people. As a child gets older and becomes accustomed to his physical environment he slowly loses some of that sensitivity. The average age at which this habituation occurs and spiritual perception fades is between eight and eleven, with normal variation, of course, because some children are naturally more sensitive than others. About 15%-20% of children retain a degree of sensitivity and grow into profoundly empathic and intuitive individuals (more on that later).

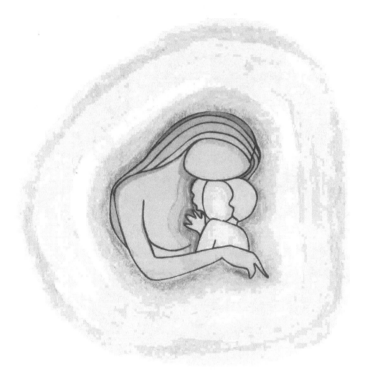

When embraced in the arms of a loving individual, the baby's energies become better organized and less chaotic. This serves to promote stable physiology (stable heart rate, breathing, temperature, etc.). The more balanced the individual is, the more harmonious the energy flow surrounding the baby.

In contrast, the baby who has yet to adapt to her physical body, becomes disorganized and energies are chaotic. Sensation is one of discomfort, therefore, the baby will cry. If embraced by a stable individual, the baby's energies will harmonize (see previous illustration). If left to cry without affection contact, the baby may commence what renowned pediatrician Dr. William Sears refers to as "Shut Down Syndrome" (see illustration in Chapter 12). More on Shut Down syndrome in the next chapter.

Another point to think about. When children of all ages are hurt, scared, or otherwise in a negative situation, most will instinctively seek out and draw up to the arms of their loving caretaker. Studies done on pain in the pediatric population show that children will have decreased pain response during uncomfortable medical procedures when a parent is warmly touching them. Touch has also been linked to improving immune function and chronic childhood illnesses like asthma. Loving, physical contact again demonstrates it organizes and harmonizes a child's mind, body, and soul.

That said, let us sum up here. A child's physiological systems are unstable and still in the process of refinement for months after she is born. Frequent and/or prolonged separation of infant and mother has been shown to send an infant into a distress mode, initiating a series of responses which are unhealthy to the body, such as the release of stress hormones. Cortisol, a major stress hormone, can suppress immune function, cause erratic breathing and heart-rate, and slow growth among other negative responses. Close contact with baby has unequivocally shown to be beneficial in terms of helping baby's physiology and emotional state. In other words, physical contact with baby helps her heart beat regularly, lungs breathe normally, temperature stabilize, and hormones balance, among many more good things. Babies are sensitive to subtle energies. Having got to this point of my book we have seen numerous indications of this truth. Would it not make perfect logic then that when embraced within the organized and stable energies of a loving individual, an infant's own energy flow would in turn respond? That close contact would enable a person's vibratory field to stimulate or synchronize with that of the child's? That the most effective catalyst for organized and healthy energy flow is the child's own mother, whose energy embraced the child during his first nine months of physical existence? One need not be a researcher to observe how loving touch possesses the power to transform.

173

Νurτurιng τhε ςoul of Our Νεω Arrιval Ωιςελψ

In the beginning half of this chapter, I mentioned the benefits of co-sleeping with your baby; better physiological functioning, exchange of sensory stimuli, some protection against SIDS, and increased intuitive response from mother, among others. *Yet the practice of co-sleeping was deemed as hazardous by the Consumer Product Safety Commission, and in September 1999 the commission issued a public warning to parents urging them to keep sleeping babies in cribs. This warning came on the heels of a CPSC study where it was found that between 1990 and 1997 five hundred and fifteen deaths of children younger than two were related to their sleeping in adult beds. Most of the deaths occurred in infants younger than three months. Of the total deaths, 121 were reported to be due to overlying of the child by an adult or sibling sleeping in the bed with the child. 394 were due to entrapment in bed railings, suffocation in soft bedding like water beds or piles of clothing or pillows, or entrapment in the bed structure such as wedging the child between the mattress and wall, bed frame, or footboard. Indeed this warning has validity. But instead of only advising parents to place infants in a crib, which seems unsound in light of the many benefits of intimate contact with baby, why not provide information on how to safely sleep with baby? Thankfully we have experts like Dr. William Sears, a renowned pediatrician and author of numerous books on the health and well-being of children, to provide solid guidelines on how to safely reap the benefits of co-sleeping with baby.

(For more information about CPSC's warning and an in-depth analysis of their data go to www.attachmentparenting.org/artresponsecpsc 2000.shtml. The article details how the study was flawed as well as misleading and perhaps culturally biased.)*

According to Dr. Sears and others, safely sleeping with baby entails the following:

* **Always** put babies younger than six months to sleep on their backs and not their tummies.

* **Do not** sleep with your baby if you are under the influence of drugs, alcohol or any substance that could diminish your awareness of your baby. Even antihistamines can impair your senses.

* **Do not** sleep with baby on soft surfaces such as bean bags, waterbeds, couches, sofas, or armchairs; nor should there be any soft items on the bed such as piles of clothing, stuffed animals or pillows that can easily suffocate baby.

* Avoid crevices between mattress and wall, or mattress and side rail. Push bed firmly against the wall and fill any cracks or empty spaces with a tightly rolled up blanket. Make sure you test the area to ensure that it will not give way to the weight of your infant.

* Avoid side rails, headboards, and footboards that have slats that can entrap baby's head. Always make sure that you are using a CPSC - approved bed rail that is completely safe.

* Avoid putting your bed near curtains or blinds that have dangling strings that could strangle baby.

* Check that the mattress size is the right fit for the bed frame. Infants can fall and get stuck between the bed and the frame if there is a gap.

* Please, one baby at a time in bed.

Much of this advice is simply common sense. One must vigilantly inspect where baby is going to sleep regardless of whether in adult bed or crib. I would like to add there are now several new wonderful options available for the family who wishes to sleep in close proximity to their young child. One is the bassinette which has an open side that faces the adult's bed. This option more or less gives you the best of both worlds. The infant sleeps in her own space in the bassinette while there is an opening on the side so she is within arm's distance of her parent(s). One bassinette of this type comes available under the marketing name of "Co-Sleeper", by Arms Reach Concepts.

Another option is a secure sleeper. This device is a ready-made mini bed intended to be placed in the center of the adult bed. It is sort of like a soft dresser drawer with mesh sides made to fit the size of a baby. This mini-bed is designed to provide a safe "nest" in which baby can sleep whereby it offers some protection against accidental parent rollover and contact with pillows or headboard. It is a nice option for those who want a little extra security while baby is in their bed.

The bottom line is that close and loving physical contact with baby provides immeasurable benefits for the health and harmony of mind, body, and soul. Western society is one of the very few in which babies are expected to sleep apart from their parents. Furthermore, throughout the day most babies are placed in fancy contraptions like bouncy baby seats, mechanical swings, and colorful playpens as opposed to being carried on the body of a loving individual in a sling or other similar device. From a vibrational stand point perhaps this is why Western people suffer more from certain illnesses, like heart disease, addictions, and certain cancers than in other societies. Remember that the seed of illness is planted long before symptoms arise. Just something to think about.

Whether Breastfeeding or Bottle Feeding:

Providing the Vibrational Benefit

Breastfeeding has been proven to be the unsurpassed way of providing nutrition to infants and young children. Human breast milk contains numerous nutritive components that are not only specific for your baby, but also *changes* and *adjusts* throughout the day to meet your baby's specific hour-by-hour needs. Indeed no one can dispute its magnificence. And when one factors in the benefits of frequent intimate contact which breastfeeding inherently provides it undoubtedly creates the optimal nourishment for baby's mind, body, and soul.

However, not all mothers can or want to breastfeed their child. It is a personal choice that should not be judged as reflective of a mother's affection and concern for her child. Some mothers simply cannot supply their child with breast milk, because their child is adopted or otherwise not their biological offspring. Though the child may not receive all the tailor-made nutrients breast milk supplies she can certainly thrive off the vibrational benefits of intimate physical contact. How does one provide the most beneficial feeding time? A time when two souls connect and the outside world fades in the background?

Whether by breastfeeding or bottle-feeding, one can create a time of "nursing" their child. Nursing a child means so much more than providing nourishment to him, it is an occasion of quiet connection that can be accomplished regardless how one chooses to feed their child. Part of the nuances which baby thrives off of when breastfeeding involves the powerful intimacy. Skin to skin contact, warm embrace, and the loving emotions of mother which baby can undoubtedly sense, all contribute to a profound nursing experience. In fact, the emotional bond between mother and child can be so powerful that simply hearing a child's cry can elicit the "let-down" response of her milk. Yet that intimacy and bonding can occur with bottle-feeding too. All that is needed is quiet time of consistent closeness when you are sharing more than a moment of feeding. You are sharing the sustenance of your heart's energy.

Your child, as in all other instances of close physical contact, can perceive the life sustaining vibrations of another loving human being. When that contact is consistently provided by someone with such powerful affections as that of a parent, feeding time also becomes an occasion for optimizing the inner workings of a child. But the benefits do rely on two key components that breastfeeding imparts. They are:

* *Consistency*; breastfeeding a child inherently means that for the most part it is being done by mother. From a vibrational stand point that signifies the child is embraced by one person's energies, and those energies are of a person with strong emotional ties to the child.

* *Close, intimate contact;* it goes without saying that breastfeeding requires close and intimate contact with baby. So when bottle-feeding, be sure to embrace the child the way one would if breastfeeding. Add to the natural warmth of this precious time of connection by allowing skin to skin contact. You can achieve this simply by wearing short sleeves or perhaps nothing on top at all. In this fast paced society, we become tempted to multi-task during this time of nourishing your baby. Some of us try to do other things while holding a bottle to our baby's mouth with an out-stretched arm, or worse yet prop the bottle up and separate entirely from baby.

Energy patterns when the child is embraced by a loving adult while feeding. Green radiance (color of the heart chakra), expands, radiates and bathes the child in vibratory sustenance. Such contact promotes intense feelings of emotional bonding and mutual serenity.

Nursing a child, whether by breast or bottle, with consistent intimate contact provides her with the vibrational benefits so essential for harmony of soul. This harmony influences the workings of her body and, as we have learned, improves her overall well-being.

Frequent close contact with baby in general promotes an intuitive bond whereby parents can respond to their child without verbal communication. You, as a parent, can anticipate what your child needs without her experiencing the negative emotions that precede crying. Parents who enjoy frequent close contact with their child have said that their intuitive bond allows them to know when their child is sick before symptoms arise. They can sense when their child has had too much stimulation, or conversely too little. They are better able to judge what activities or situations are best for their child. Parents who know their child deeply can wisely discern the best way to discipline him or her, for there is not one effective method for each unique child. Being keenly aware of both their strengths and weaknesses, they may also better steer their child toward areas in which they would naturally succeed. But perhaps most important comes a confidence in knowing that you are nurturing your child in a way that is magnificently specific for her. So specific, that no parenting book or advice from well-meaning friends can ever reign superior over your own powerful instinct, made possible through a soul to soul connection.

Indeed, our children are dependent on their caretakers for more than food, protection, and love. As a spiritual being new to physicality they are intricately needy of connecting with the part of us that offers timeless recognition, our souls. Embraced in the resonance of someone who loves her incredibly and unconditionally, can you think of any more powerful force for health? I certainly cannot.

Chapter Twelve

Nurturing for the Health and Harmony of

Our Children's Inner Being

"We cannot prepare for the future without embracing the meaning and the relevance of the baby's perspective on life."

Michel Odent, MD

Pick up any one of the dozen or so magazines on parenting issues and chances are you will see an article about "how to get your baby to sleep". It has surely become a challenge which Western society feels it must conquer. Logical of a fast paced society we tend always to look for a convenient and time saving solution. Consequently a batch of "experts" appear whose purpose is to teach parents how to do just that: get their baby to sleep when they want , where they want, with very little flexibility outside that routine. This sleep training promises that you can simply put your child down, and basically be free to go on about your business. Whether that be to have a good night's sleep yourself or to catch up on some work. Yes, tempting indeed. Add to this the expectation of children as young as a day to sleep in a separate bed in a separate room where every occasion to comfort him increasingly becomes an exhausting task. Ah, please tell me the name of the sleep training book, I will buy it tomorrow! Indeed, we have been setting ourselves up for such methods to be desirable.

But what if we reframe the ideal environment for young children? What if instead of concentrating so much on a fancily decorated nursery room, we focus on ways to have our child closer to us, because it is proven best? Instead of that big designer crib you saw in a stylish advertisement, you search for an open sided bassinette so baby will be next to you, within arm's reach, throughout the night. And that your expectations for your child to transition to her own bed in her own room lie on *her* readiness, not *yours*. Does that sound backwards to you? Perhaps even primitive in this progressive world we live in, where we strive for abundance which includes having a separate space for everyone in the family? Or does it sound like a freeing thought, the idea that parents would be expected to keep baby close to them for the first few years of life? Why would it not be an absolute liberating thought? Doing so would mean no more having to get up and schlep to another room numerous times for an unhappy baby. It would mean greater ease in caring for baby throughout the night. Happier healthier baby, better and longer sleep for you. It would mean establishing an intuitive bond with baby, so you would not have to awaken fully to know what baby needs.

Still, there will be parents who simply wish to have their child separated from them for whatever reason, which would logically make sleep training a desirable option. It would eliminate the task of getting up frequently to parent their child to sleep each night. Convenient yes, except for one thing, *there are reasons why young children have a difficult time going to sleep,* because of their immature physiology and newness to physical existence.

Envision this. You are a timeless being just having been born. The onslaught of new sensations is almost overwhelming in itself. Still you discover another challenge, your new body functions in an unorganized manner because it has not yet synchronized with the forces of your magnificent soul. You realize that you need help to organize it, you need the soothing comfort of being within the aura of a loving person. Once your body becomes slightly more organized, after a few weeks of being born, you are now more alert to your environment. Your sensations have become sharper, you are hungrier, thirstier, and can keenly perceive the slightest discomfort. Sleep is a frightening surrender of whatever little control and understanding of your surroundings you have earned. You enter it lightly because you need to know that your adult is nearby, available to reach out and help you when you need her, which will inevitably be soon because you cannot go long without a refill of sustenance, both nutritional and vibratory. You know that waking up frequently is not only good for your development, but it is a survival tactic.

Let us go further and imagine two dramatically different approaches to getting a child to sleep. Once again you are that baby. While awake your senses were stimulated with noises, smells, colors, touch, you name it. You are tired but your inner self feels more chaotic than ever. You need *help* to get to sleep. You need the comfort and safety of knowing you can let go and surrender to it. You instinctively seek that sensation of loving intent which usually comes from close contact with mother. This close contact also helps body and soul synchronize, and your inner self will be soothed and work in a more orderly manner. Your caregiver responds by embracing you, rocking you to a lullaby, and placing you beside her to nurse (breast or bottle). She stays with you until your physical body relaxes and its systems move smoothly in synchronization creating the comfort and security that is the essential prelude to sleep. Feeling safe you finally let go of the control that your young physical body has demanded of you. Sometimes you will even place your body in a way so that the top of your head is resting against something, so that your entire self remains integrated and nothing escapes. It also instills the security felt during those last days (or minutes), in the womb with head against the birthing canal. You awake several minutes or hours later. The rush of sensations wash over your new body. It is still unfamiliar and chaos again ensues within your entire body. Knowing no other way to communicate your discomfort, you cry. Thank goodness your loving adult is nearby to once again embrace your startled self. You drift off in a blur of perceptive affection, love, and security.

Now let us envision a scene quite different. One that is consistent with so-called sleep-training methods for children. You are again that tired but stimulated baby mentioned above. You need help to surrender to sleep, yet instead of a warm embrace you are placed in a cold crib by yourself. You immediately perceive something is wrong, that the help you need to quiet the chaos inside you is not available. You do the only thing you can do to alert your caregiver, you cry. Only instead of a response you get empty silence. No embrace to sooth your soul or help coordinate your inner workings. You cry more but sooner or later realize no one is coming, or when they do come it is only to pat your back and leave once again. As you continue crying your discomfort and chaos increases until something strange happens, you realize the necessity to stop. In order to conserve precious energy you must "shut down". Eventually, after shutting down you surrender to sheer exhaustion, not secure calm. And after many nights of the same routine of caregiver absence you learn how to shut down quicker so that your energy remains conserved to carry out its most basic functions. You do whatever it takes to substitute that comforting presence, you place your fingers in your mouth or you snuggle up against a small stuffed animal. Yet nothing will adequately substitute for that human presence. The loss of energy creates a sense of lasting emptiness, and you have essentially learned on a deep level that you cannot trust your environment. Perhaps you will grow to unconsciously seek fulfillment of that emptiness. Maybe food, drugs, alcohol, or relationships based on dependence will work to temporarily fill that void.

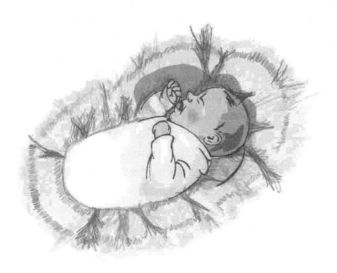

What happens to the baby's energy when it undergoes "Shut -Down Syndrome". Shut-Down Syndrome is a term used by Dr. William Sears that describes a type of failure to thrive seen in young children. Spiritually, weakening of the body's energies are due to prolonged and excessive crying with extreme energy loss. Self-preservation of the child involves diminished responsiveness over time with repeated episodes of such energy loss. Lasting energy dysfunction is likely to ensue. Outwardly, the child will often become emotionally withdrawn, despondent, and may cease thriving.

Indeed, it is no surprise that lack of coping skills and harmful addictions were found in people whose fundamental needs for closeness were not met by a loving individual. And as I alluded to in my last chapter I suspect the consequences of our distant-type of parenting young children has further reaching health implications, like our susceptibility to heart disease and other illnesses. Not to mention rearing a child with little or no empathy, compassion, or intuition of their own. Always bear in mind that illness begins with disharmony way before symptoms arise. It is entirely possible, if not likely, that the disharmony begins in early childhood.

I know I have said this numerous times, but there are *reasons* babies cry for comfort before going to sleep and sometimes upon awakening based on their inter-relationship between physiological, psychological, and spiritual. It involves a simple dependence on that which connects us all, the human soul. And because of the wide variation in terms of their uniqueness, I cannot place an age at which you can expect your child to become more secure in his surrender to sleep. You must try to sense your baby's individual level of trepidation in letting go. Thus intuitive nurturing becomes vital in assisting him in a way NO parenting advice can. How do you intuit your child's inner being? As broached in Chapter 10, the steps are:

1 - While you are alone with your baby, close your eyes and temporarily forget every child rearing advice you received from *anyone,* including family members, physicians, parenting experts, etc.. Do this as often as you can, undisturbed with the intent on connecting with your child.

2 - Look, listen, and feel your baby; then sense the radiance of his beautiful life force. What does it feel like when he is calm? Try to sense the difference in his essence when he is calm/alert and calm/sleepy. What about when he begins to cry? What does the intensity of his chaotic energy flow tell you? Do you

sense the sharpness of pain, or the dullness of discomfort? The vast majority of times when a healthy baby cries it is because he is expressing the discomfort of his frenzied spirit as it adapts to the physical body. And when he is becoming ill his essence will communicate that as well. People who practice intuitive nurturing with their child report being able to discern when he or she is getting sick, *even before symptoms occur*. Personally, I have had many experiences with my children when I have taken them to the physician because I knew something infectious was brewing. When the practitioner asked what symptoms led to my suspicion I would not know what to say. It was not that she had cries of discomfort, lethargy, fever, loss of appetite, or anything else objective to observe in terms of symptoms. I had simply sensed a change in my child when I held her close to me, a change in the workings of her inner body. It might have felt like a speeding up of her energies, or a certain alteration than I would normally feel when I held her. Sometimes the illness was not yet evident upon examination, and I would be sent home only to frustratingly return a couple of days later with my child suffering from full blown symptoms. I have heard and witnessed the same story from many other parents who are intuitively connected to their children. And when that bond does occur it can be one of the most liberating feelings you will have as a parent.

3 - *Obey your own soul's natural instinct to embrace your child.* I cannot emphasize this enough. A child's cries are designed to evoke a physical response from you, however it is your baby's last resort of communication. Notice the change in his entire little being when you hold him close to your heart. Suddenly his body relaxes, conserving precious physical energy. His soul is soothed, harmonizing the form and flow of his inner workings. Remember, by familiarizing yourself to your baby's unique spiritual dynamics you will be able to intuit what your baby needs or wants *before* he has to cry. Bear in

mind that "slow-to-adapt" or "sensitive" children logically take longer to feel the security of surrendering to sleep. This all relates to their new but very intense perception of physical life.

And yes, there will be the concerns like, what if baby gets used to sleeping with parent(s)? What about when the couple wants to have sex in the room where baby is? All I can say is that you *want* the child to get used to the *security* of sleeping with parents. Once the child's need for security diminishes, (and trust me it WILL diminish), she will readily transition to her own space. It is when she feels *insecure* that she will continue to seek the security of your space. When the adult couple wants to have intimate private time there are ways and other places to get fun and creative. My husband and I enjoy our time together after the children are asleep. Believe me, the creativity and spontaneity of making that private time happen can be an exciting part of the foreplay!

NURTURING THE UNIQUE SOUL OF BABY

Everybody is unique. And that uniqueness is present in each upon birth with diverse temperaments, likes, dislikes, and gifts. In terms of disposition, the more challenging to parents are the infants who are "fussy", "sensitive", or "colic". They enter our world with a rawness of their souls, displaying such a sensitivity as if to be saying "being alive is uncomfortable".

These children are the ones who will experience severe separation and stranger anxiety, and tend to be comforted only by their mother. As they grow older, these children may respond negatively to some rather traditional approaches to parenting. Providing discipline and guidance seems to only be effective if carried out with the utmost of love and affection. These children often cannot be "trained" to go to sleep, nor will they positively respond to any type of detached instruction.

(Personally, when describing a child, I loathe the terms "difficult", or when people ask if your child is a "good baby". *All* children are "good", it is simply an issue of whether he has the support and understanding of his beautifully unique inner self. The more appropriate question for the caretaker is, "are *you* good?")

Each of these children have the same underlying cause for their emotional and physical behavior. They are experiencing a challenging adaptation to their physical reality. These are the children who arrive and approach body and soul integration with great difficulty. Their inner beings may be highly sensitive to their physical environment thus requiring plenty of assistance and nurturing which goes beyond physical and emotional needs; that is the need for nurturing of their soul.

Colic in itself is defined loosely as excessive crying in a child who is not easily consoled. The crying is usually not related to any pathology, meaning there is no abnormality of the structure or function of the child's body, nor is there infection of any kind. The only two exceptions to this finding include the infant having an allergy to cow's milk (whether through formula, or through breast milk by which the cow's milk was ingested by mother), or the infant having a medical condition called Gastro-esophageal Reflux (acid indigestion). For infants who have the allergy to cow's milk a simple omission, or decrease consumed by the breastfeeding mother can alleviate most of baby's discomfort. For the formula fed baby a switch to one which does not have cow's milk will usually do the trick. Gastro-esophageal Reflux (GER) can be relieved by positioning the infant in a thirty degree angle while on his belly for thirty minutes after a feeding. Offering baby smaller, more frequent feedings can also help the baby with GER. (For more information on whether your baby has GER, and the current treatments available please see your pediatric practitioner. For an excellent pediatric resource to learn about GER and other children's issues, I highly recommend the website of Dr. William Sears and his wife Martha Sears, RN, **www.askdrsears.com.** Simply type in GER in the search field.)

One prevailing theory among researchers regarding the origins of colic is what I mentioned in my last chapter, the belief that the infant's immature and disorganized physiology is a major influence to the development of colic. Or, as I would say in very simple words, their keen sensitivity to life as a physical being.

And yes, as I have been saying all along, there are some babies who are simply more reactive and/or slower to adapt to their new physical life than others. These babies require even more hands-on help to place their energies in order. The symptoms of colic, including GER, in my opinion all stem from one thing: an exceptionally unorganized and chaotic inner being.

Two of my children, my second and third, went through this phase of inconsolable crying at about 2 - 3 months of age which lasted about eight weeks. The episodes would begin in the early evening and last until the late evening. I distinctly remember the particulars of my first experience with my second son because I painfully did not know what I know now. I recall not being able to eat dinner with my husband and my three year old, because whenever anyone else but me would try to hold my second son, his screams would just escalate. Because I was a young mother I remember feeling like a failure, clearly I was not caring for him adequately if he was in so much pain. Pediatricians advised me that the "colic" would pass and suggested giving him simethicone drops for intestinal gas which they thought may be causing him additional abdominal discomfort. The drops did not work, nor did changing my diet to see if he was sensitive to something that was passing through my breast milk. I read everything I could about colic only to be left feeling absolutely helpless, as everything I read suggested I find solace in knowing it will soon pass. But that advice was not acceptable for me because I *knew* from the intensity of my baby's screams that he was indeed in *pain.*

Then one day as I was looking for a way to clean my two story home while keeping my colicky son Ethan in sight I pulled out an infant carrier which was given to me as a gift for my baby shower. I strapped Ethan to my chest and went about cleaning the house. That dreaded dinner time was soon approaching, but since Ethan was so calm and quiet in the carrier I kept him there while I began to prepare the food. Then something dramatic happened. He did not cry at the usual time of his bouts. There on my chest he was calm and serene, so much so that it was palpable. Could I have been on to something? Could Ethan's episodes of colic actually disappear by simply placing him in an infant carrier for a good part of the day? My husband and I dared not wish such an uncomplicated solution. So I took one day at a time wearing him on my chest. And marvelously, that tranquility would last into the evening if I wore him long enough during the day. Yes, at times wearing him all day on my chest was exhausting, but it was a million times better than experiencing the episodes of his incessant crying.

At that point in my life I did not yet understand what I know now about the unique challenges our babies face as they grow. In retrospect it all makes perfect sense. Ethan is an extremely sensitive child who, at his present age of eleven, still needs me very close at hand to help his sense of security and orderliness. If I am physically next to him he can think clearer and display an overall disposition of increased integrity and ease. (In Chapter 13, I will provide tips on how to help your reactive child feel more secure in his environment).

Have you ever seen a baby in the throes of a colic episode? It is absolutely nerve shattering and it provokes the most extreme sense of helplessness in the caregiver I have ever experienced. Baby suddenly stiffens his body, arches his back,

191

and then begins screaming. As he continues to scream he lifts his knees up toward his abdomen as though doubling up in pain, giving the appearance that the source of his misery is coming from his stomach. This is where the term "colic" originates for it literally means "stomach pain". His abdomen becomes tense and subsequently bloated as air goes in from the incessant crying, inevitably adding to his discomfort. Every part of you knows he is hurting and perhaps instinctively you place a hand on his belly to soothe him. But at this point there is little you can do to stop this misery that both of you now share.

Yet, I will tell you that based on the structure and function of the infant's chaotic energies and subsequent physiologic workings, mother's wisdom and instincts about where their child's pain comes from is absolutely accurate. For colic arises in the infant at a very significant point of the body, the solar plexus. It is the region of the body where the physical integrates and unifies with the spiritual; it reflects the soul's process of adjustment to her new environment. In other words, colic *is* the manifestation of the challenges in which the soul experiences as it is joining and adapting to its body.

The naked character and energetic subtleties of the child's inner being is what determines whether she will approach this acclimation with difficulty or ease. There are children who display little, if any, difficulty adjusting to their environment. I guess this is the child one would call a "good baby". These children readily adjust to their new environment, their transition is smooth and for that reason they appear calm and content. They do not require as much "hands-on" help from a mother figure as the sensitive child; they can easily be held in the arms of both family and strangers alike without a fuss. The flow of their inner selves is not as chaotic, therefore they do not fuss because of internal discomfort.

The other extreme is the baby with colic who is hurting. They require special assistance to calm the chaos inside, to help them adjust and feel more secure and complete. Therefore, the kind of nurturing the child receives is crucial to whether that child will establish inner harmony early, or continue to hurt until desensitization inevitably occurs. This is where we see how certain child raising tactics can actually be harmful to a child's healthy development. This is also where we can easily see how and why intimate contact with a child can 1) reduce symptoms of colic; 2) calm a "fussy" baby; 3) help baby's breathing, heart rate, blood pressure, and temperature; 4) improve her immune system; 5) improve baby's sleep; 6) possibly guard against SIDS; and of course, 7) enhance her emotional well-being with a greater sense of love, security, and integrity. Baby's abdomen contains the message of whether she is handling her arrival well.

Let us see what else we can do to effectively help her:

* *Infant Massage*: Place baby on her back with the soles of her feet facing you. Rub some warm massaging oil (unscented or very lightly scented; can even be olive oil) between your hands and place your hands on baby's belly. In a circular clock-wise motion begin moving your hand with gentle pressure around your baby's abdomen. You will have to experiment with how much pressure to place because too little may tickle baby, and of course, you would want to avoid applying too much pressure. You can also alternate your hand movements between circular movements and strokes in the shape of a 7.

You may even try doing these movements with your hand about an inch away from her skin as this would work to move the energy of your baby's middle. Both methods can be very effective and beneficial for baby. Getting about five minutes of this loving touch is ideal. And obviously, if baby complains louder while performing the massage, do stop. She may be already too stimulated.

* *Wear baby* in a carrying device for at least three hours a day: Anthropologists who study child rearing around the world have long recognized how babies who are held in a carrier the majority of the day cry far less than those who are not. And in a 1986 study done in Montreal pediatricians revealed that babies who were carried cried and fussed 43% less than those in the non-carried group. Once again giving credence to the premise of a child's dependence on the essence of his caretaker. Close contact with the subtle flow of his mother (or other main caretaker) helps to organize and stabilize baby's inner workings of spirit, and thus his body.

* *Hold baby*: Certain positions are more effective than others in relieving the cries. Those that apply gentle pressure to the abdomen such as the football hold (draping baby face down along the length of your arm with her head against the inside bend of your elbow), or placing baby face down on your chest while laying down with her head up against the curve of your throat and chin.

* *Soothing music or lullabies*: Yes, music *can* comfort the soul.

* *Frequent feedings*: Intimate time lovingly embraced while rhythmically sucking can often quiet the most frenzied of souls.

* Whatever else, you (as the parent or caretaker) can intuit your child needs. I will say this a dozen times, the moment you get behind your child's eyes and connect with her essence you will have access to her "owner's manual". There will be no other advice that can match what you sense of your child. What she wants and needs are communicable via the powerful bond of love. Trust your intuition, and know you can respond unequivocally to your baby's most unseen needs.

Alas, I must caution you. Despite following this guidance toward achieving intuitive nurturing, it is entirely possible that no matter what you do, your baby will simply have an exceptionally difficult time transitioning to her new existence. Some babies have to make sense of it all and work it out on their own. Having an intense crying session for certain babies may initiate a release and re-alignment of their energy, which is a beneficial thing. This occurred with my youngest, who was also colicky for many weeks. Even with carrying her most of the day, performing infant massage, and playing soothing music she still had a day or two of intense crying. But here is the difference, I *knew* she needed that good cry. I stayed next to her, made sure she was not hurt or sick and watched her entire body tense up then release, followed by a profound calmness and serenity. I understood that there was nothing I could do to help her achieve that release; she needed to let go of that energy on her own. If this seems to be the case with your little one just please ensure that she is safe before allowing her a good cry. And always have someone present ready to embrace her when she is finished.

Which brings me to my last point. Having a child with colic can take a dramatic toll on your role as a loving and responsive parent. It can make you question your ability and *desire* to nurture your own child. As I mentioned earlier the crying can be unnerving, and when the baby is calmed only by one person, usually the mother, the emotional weight sustained by that one person is huge. For your emotional health get as much assistance as you possibly can. There is no amount of instinct better than the awareness of the limits of your own being. When you have had enough, recognize it and allow someone else to share in the "joys" of parenting your expressive child. Because once you have reached a point of distress you will only add momentum to what your baby is already experiencing. You and baby will need a break from one another. Once you have restored your own inner harmony, only then can you help your baby find her own.

We have been allowing a form of parenting in this society that counterintuitive. Our rushed pace and hectic lifestyles with increasing technology to streamline it all sets us up to look for ways to make our lives even more efficient. Subsequently, certain trends in parenting appear. Sleep-training, crying it out, scheduled feedings, and all forms of this distant-type of parenting have led, I believe, to generations of children who lack empathy, basic trust, and their own intuition. And by continuing to allow this detachment we fail in providing our children with the internal well-being needed to grow to be healthy and nurturing individuals. Our children need to be raised with the wisdom of our minds, the strength of our bodies, and the loving brilliance of our soul. Nurture that soul to soul union with your baby and witness a potential that is both unmatched and fantastically glorious. Not only for your child but for you as well.

Chapter Thirteen

The Blossoming of a Fulfilled Essence

"What's done to children, they will do to society."

Karl Menninger

When I took my daughter to her fourth month well-baby checkup she was seen by my practitioner's associate. Three minutes or so into our visit and in a very matter-of-fact manner he began advising me on how to put my baby to sleep, never once bothering to ask if I needed or wanted this advise. "Make sure you put her down in her crib while she's still awake so she gets used to soothing herself." Well Doc, why don't we just throw you in the middle of the ocean, watch you struggle for a while, and then toss you a life vest only when we see you're on the brink of drowning, just because we think this is how you should learn to swim? But, of course, being the patient and respectful person that I am, I simply told him that I had no issues in that area because I co-slept with my baby. Up went his eyebrows just before giving me that "I pity you" look on his face. Was that slight blow to my self-assurance as a mother intentional, Doc?

Then I went on to share how my sensitive little one would cry in the arms of anyone other than me, and how she did not tolerate separation well. This doc turned to me with a smirk and sarcastically said, "Well, then maybe she's super advanced for her age, because stranger and separation anxiety shouldn't come for another several months." Did you just mock me as though I were ignorant, Doc? Was that another suggestion that I could not

197

possibly know more than you about my own daughter?

In what seemed to be a final attempt to chisel away some of my mothering confidence he scoffed at the idea of my dabbing numbing cream on my daughter's arm to minimize the pain from the needle of the vaccination he was due to give her. I emerged from that doctor's visit with my self-assurance as a mother temporarily shaken. I could not help but wonder if that was this physician's intent. Did he assume that by being our pediatrician it placed him in the role of being an authoritative figure on parenting, which commanded compliance? No, I happen to know for a fact that medical school does not offer a sub-specialty in parenting. And even if it did, the instinctual bond between parent and child is one that deserves respect, not polite patronizing.

My second son, Ethan, is an exceptionally sensitive child. As a student approaching junior high school he is met daily with challenges that could break his spirit. Year after school year I am called into meetings with his teachers, school social worker, and psychologist because his sensitivities interfere with his capacity to learn in a regular class environment. His needs are so unique that modifications for his education must be tailored for him alone. I have spent the majority of Ethan's life trying to understand what it is like to be him. Thankfully, the wonderful staff at his school has recognized my hard-earned insight of his vulnerable nature, and often requests my input so that together a plan can be developed to help him to succeed. I have offered tips on how to reduce his level of arousal, and how to redirect him when he seems overwhelmed. Because of this cohesive approach my son is thriving in school; so much so that he has achieved honors during several semesters.

Ethan is in fact a huge inspiration to the creation of this book. His arrival to our family *forced* me to put down the books written by "experts", and parent with the wisdom of my soul as well as my mind. He and his sister officially shattered the idea of some stranger who knows nothing about my child having the capacity of being an "expert" on parenting them. Their powerful individuality broke my pride of being a well-read mother who also studied child psychology in college. Oh, how I thought I knew it all.

Brandon, my first born, endured the cross of my arrogance. Being a new and insecure mother I fanatically poured over the parenting books striving to be perfectly educated in the science of child-rearing. I fed my son on schedule. I considered the advice of not holding him for very long as the thought was that he would become too accustomed to being comforted in someone's arms. At that time, it was understood as being a hindrance toward a child's development of independence. I trained him to sleep as a six month infant on his own. I allowed my son to cry for me and not respond, despite the fact that I almost felt my spirit jump out of my skin to hold him.

But that's what the "experts" said I should do. I was proficient in the science of parenting, only to learn that in the end raising children is NOT a science. It is about the art of bringing out what is divine, unique, and magnificently purposeful in this gift from God. As a young child, my beautiful boy tolerated his mother raising him with a mind that was "book-smart" but with a soul that was silenced and, consequently, a heart that learned limits. I surrendered my own inner wisdom born of connecting with my son's soul, in lieu of the illusion that someone knew more about my boy than I.

I would do almost anything to bring back Brandon's young childhood and do it over. During the last ten years or so we have seen the emergence of a somewhat insecure boy. Despite our telling him what an intelligent, warm, and funny kid he is he does not seem to believe it. While observing him in social situations we often find him trying to be somebody he is not.

Could I say with certainty that my rigid and detached style of parenting had anything to do with my older son's current insecurity? No I cannot. But if I would have obeyed my instincts as his mother one hundred percent of the time, at least I would have the solace of knowing that it did not. I can now only try to catch up lost time and try my best to nurture his self-doubting soul.

Am I suggesting you ignore information produced by these knowledgeable people in the hugely complex subject of parenting? **Of course not.** As I mentioned earlier in this book *gather as much information as you possibly can as you journey along your role as a parent.* If your child is colicky, learn as much as you can about it. If your child is exceptionally shy, research as much as you possibly can. If your child sucks her thumb until the age of nine, find information about that as well. And so on. *Educate yourself on the science of what may apply to your child, but then master the art of knowing your child's individual spirit.* What is appropriate or relevant for some children may not be for yours. Tune into her soul by knowing enough about her so that you may get behind her eyes. Could it be that your child's shyness is actually beneficial for her, and not detrimental like so much literature suggests? Might the fact that your child is sucking her thumb be telling you something important that she is unable to verbalize? This is the heart of Intuitive Nurturing.

I share these stories because as I near the end of this book I want to firmly communicate the grace and power of your own instincts when it comes to your child. Even well-meaning professionals cannot possibly know what you as the parent have precious perception of. Yes, when it comes to the science of practicing a specific skill, leave that to the professionals such as educators or healthcare practitioners. But always know that you are the professional on your child, which has an important role in the application of that skill. Such advocacy can make differences that last a lifetime.

Providing the Wind for Their Sails

Young children require all that encompasses close loving contact. The warmth of their mother's embrace, the touch of their father's playful hand, and the radiance of their parent's heart. Not just for their emotional health, but for their physical, mental, and spiritual well-being children need to be bathed in the invisible vibrations of pure love. It is proven time and again that something miraculous happens when they are simply held close by someone who loves them. And the more physical affection happens, the better it is for all involved.

However, the dependence your child has on the loving and vibrational bonds you share vary widely from one child to the next. Some children simply need the security it provides more than others. Even identical twins can display a wide difference in their level of need for sustenance of the soul. Typically, as a child gets older and becomes accustomed to his physical environment he can rely less on these vibrational bonds. The average age at which this occurs is between eight and eleven, with normal variation, of course.

Highly sensitive children, however, are an exception. According to Elaine Aron, Ph.D. and bestselling author of *The Highly Sensitive Child* about 15%-20% of children are highly sensitive and remain so throughout their adult lives. These are the children I mentioned earlier that can be very reactive, fussy or colicky babies. They are born simply needing an exceptionally responsive-type of parenting to help them adapt to life. With a sensitive child, there is no average age at which they grow less needy of the security of their caregiver's vibrational sustenance. The parenting goal then becomes providing the support, security, love, guidance, and tools for your child to tap into when she feels her sensitivity to physical life overwhelming her.

Hence, sensitive or not, what can do parents do to help their children soar? As I have said earlier I believe success is defined as one's sense of fulfillment in life. Success in any endeavor means little if fulfillment is not achieved. But in order to find fulfillment one must be capable of accessing the part of themselves that seeks completion; that inner peace which can only be achieved through self-actualization. What cultivates self-actualization? The first step is, of course, the recognition of the child's radiant inner being, which is beautifully unique. His talents, his abilities, and yes, even his shortcomings. In other words the child's *innateness*. A child who achieves this self-actualization, alignment of soul with mind and body, unleashes their full potential and purpose on this universe, which so greatly needs him.

Innateness is immediately evident in the newborn. I would like you to try this exercise if you are already a parent, or have a young child in your life.

1) Try to recall the earliest demonstration of the child's temperament. Was she serene and unbothered by the newness of activity around her? Or was she aware of the slightest stimulation and highly reactive to her environment? These are glimpses into her innateness, the disposition of her soul that will likely remain with her throughout her life.

2) Look at pictures taken within his first year of life. What do you see? Does the camera capture natural gestures of apprehension or outright fearlessness? What can the child's eyes tell you in the photo? Do you see the soft look of a calm nature, or the fiery look of an intense spirit? Pictures taken in the first year of life are usually spontaneous and unposed images which can reveal the inner essence of the child. As the old saying goes, "A picture is worth a thousand words", and this certainly holds true for what a photo can express about our children's spirit.

3) What natural loves, abilities, talents, and aversions did she have? I will never forget how my daughter as a four month old baby would rock back and forth to the slightest rhythm. She could

barely lift her head up, yet she was swaying to the beat of any song playing in the background. A natural affinity to music was something that resonated in my daughter's soul. Note too a child's aversions. I know of young children who cannot handle competition well; it brings about an extreme response of stress and anxiety. Obviously then as they grow these children may not fare well participating in highly competitive sports.

An important role of parenting would then be to recognize the powerful spirit in the child, accentuate his strengths, and soften his weaknesses. No expectations of what your child should be, based on you or any other member of the family. Child-rearing then becomes a customized endeavor for each individual child, regardless of how many children you are raising. Such things as guidance, discipline, and even praise, have its own special role as we learn to tailor each specifically for the individual child. An outgoing twelve year old child with a rich social life might necessitate different guidance, discipline, and praise than her introverted sister at that age who is a real homebody. Allow me to provide an example.

Maria has two daughters, ages 14 and 12. Though raised by the same mother and father they are complete opposites in character. Brianna, the 14 year old, is an outgoing popular child with many friends who loves sports and extracurricular activities. In fact, Maria often complains that Brianna is hardly ever home, always being at either a sport practice, rehearsal, or just hanging out with friends. She has a natural ease in learning new things and is an honor student. Yet with all her smarts, she is not very intuitive or empathetic, which often frustrates Maria because of her lack of patience with her sister, Eliza.

Eliza, Maria's 12 year old, is entirely different. She is a very sensitive child who is introverted, loves being at home, and has only one or two close friends. She hates sports and has not done well with extracurricular activities, despite her parent's encouragement to become involved. Eliza's favorite past-time is playing video games alone in her room. She struggles for every decent grade she gets, and at times absolutely needs a "mental-health" day off from school because of being so overwhelmed.

Maria and her husband were under the impression that parenting should always be equal in terms of providing their children with guidance, discipline, and praise; what applies for one must apply for the other. But over the years of parenting such opposites they have learned that indeed what works for one did either nothing or too much for the other. As young children, Brianna needed strict disciplining where she would get a time-out for misbehaving. Yet when Eliza would require disciplining, giving her the same time-out would elicit a horrific emotional meltdown where Maria became afraid the child might hurt herself. Maria quickly learned that all Eliza really needed to correct a behavior was a stern look or the removal of what they regarded as a "privilege" such as movie-time or game-playing time. Doing the same for Brianna would never work because she did not care as much for those past-times. Yet something felt incredibly unfair about giving one child time-out and not the other. In fact, Brianna often accused her mother and father of playing "favorites", because she thought Eliza's punishments were light.

The same "inequality" applied to guidance and praise. Maria and her husband found the need to teach Brianna how to be sensitive to other people's feelings, as she would at times display a crass sense of humor. Not so for Eliza, who even pointed out whenever her parents were thoughtless. But when it came to daily functioning Eliza was the one who required constant and consistent guidance. Because she was so easily overwhelmed Eliza would often experience bouts of forgetfulness, where Maria would have to remind and reinforce simple day to day instruction.

Praise was another facet of parenting that was slightly uneven when it came to these two sisters. Maria and her husband, of course, lavished both girls with praise when appropriate, but somehow Eliza needed more to sustain her. Brianna was always a confident child earning admiration from many for her intelligence and skills. Eliza, however, seemed to always be the "odd one", who was always painfully aware of her differences. Therefore, Maria and her husband found themselves often having to point out her strengths simply to have her gain a healthy sense of self-worth.

So you see, from distant perspective, it might seem as though these parents are unfairly treating their children differently. One gets harsher discipline than the other, one receives greater guidance than the other, and even praise is slightly unbalanced between the two sisters. But this is exactly what each required in order to thrive, because of their individual uniqueness. If this is the case in your home, it is imperative that you be open and honest with each child as to the reason why their sibling has an adjusted form of parenting. Brianna's belief that her mother was playing "favorites" with Eliza was very real and emotionally painful for her. Maria had to help Brianna understand that Eliza was indeed being disciplined, just in a manner that would work for her.

Helping your children to achieve fulfillment in life goes beyond providing love and protection. Fulfillment in life means becoming aware of your inborn magnificence and walking a path in life that illuminates that greatness, something in which parents and all others in a position of guidance can help foster in our children. Children are born unto this world with the essence of their naked soul filled with universal purpose. It is subsequently the nurturing he or she receives and experiences that influences their personality, and thus their sense of alignment with their inner greatness. We, as adults guiding our children, cannot, of course, control their every experience. Nor would we want to, for much has reason, beyond our knowledge, to be lain on their individual life path. But what we can do is our best to recognize and honor that innateness they came into this world with.

How many times do we hear of parents influencing their children to do or be something that *they wish for themselves?* A parent's preconceived notion of how their child should be, or an unfulfilled desire of their own can often shroud the child's true distinctiveness. What often ends up happening is the child's sense of his authentic self becomes distorted or confused. The child develops into a person the *mind believes* he should be, creating misalignment with his soul. The energies of the body follow with this disharmony, setting the foundation for what I detailed in the first part of this book: dysfunctional and disease-creating flow.

Or sometimes, we as adults make the mistake of seeing what is actually a strength of their individuality as a fault or weakness. Say your child is exceptionally tenacious and unbending. He seems to question your very authority as his parent. What may outwardly seem as stubbornness and adversarial can actually be displaying a child who is passionate, judicious, and strong-willed. It is simply a matter of perspective. If we nurture those traits in the context of being advantageous, as opposed to trying to suppress them, we facilitate bringing out what is divine in them.

Another example is shyness. What may seem as timidity or lack of courage may instead be a healthy response of pausing to thoroughly perceive their environment before proceeding. And possessing the innate tendency to "pause-to-check" is certainly a benefit. Your so-called shy daughter may cling to your leg whenever she is in an unfamiliar situation, but that same cautiousness can serve to protect her from getting into unsafe situations in the future. Take note of each child's innateness, nurture the positive nature of their traits, and watch as their magnificence unfolds.

We are all responsible for taking on this role of empowerment for our children. Parents, educators, coaches, healthcare professionals, and anyone who has a child in their life. For it may be the smallest of experiences that dramatically shape a child's life. How often do we hear of the power one teacher, one coach, or one grandmother had in greatly influencing a child's life? We are *all* responsible for the greatness of our young generation, regardless of our relation to them.

SENSITIVE, INDIGO, AND CRYSTAL CHILDREN: ARE THEY THE ESSENCES OF SPIRITUAL PROGRESSION?

All living things evolve. A gradual development of the organism into something more complex and advanced. It is what we humans have done since our arrival on this Earth approximately five million years ago. The body evolves by passing on genetic material which is favorable for its environment. This is the nature of our success in terms of survival as a species.

Yet humans have gone beyond basic survival, our minds have progressed to the point of outstanding achievements. The brilliance of one discovery is followed by many in the same area. Technology in today's age alone progresses at an amazingly rapid rate. What is considered new is no longer just six months later.

Intelligence is said to be housed in the brain. What's more, the brain is the organ of the mind, the center of consciousness. Thoughts, attitudes, feelings, ideas, and perceptions are all processed within the mind. Yet we know for certain the human mind is not the product of simple genetic makeup passed down to our offspring. It contains that part which we have discussed and science cannot explain, innateness. The mind is the vehicle through which the soul expresses itself, and as such it is affected by our Creator. It follows then that human progression is guided by an energy far greater than any life form. In what direction is our spirit, nudged by God, taking us?

The concept of spiritual evolution is not a novel one. It is an idea shared and pursued by the philosophical, the theological, and esoteric. So after pursuing my own knowledge of the ideation of spiritual evolution it actually came as no surprise that there were, in fact, some obvious parallels between the concepts presented in several modern-day works. Dr. Paul H. Ray and Dr. Sherry Ruth Anderson speak of "Cultural Creatives", who are part of a growing population that will offer, "A more hopeful future and prepare us all for a transition to a new, saner, and wiser culture." In their book *The Cultural Creatives*, published in the year 2000, these authors present evidence of a diverse group of people who, with their profoundly spiritual and altruistic nature, are slowly changing the world we live in. They are concerned with authenticity, whole process learning (meaning enhanced with intimacy and instinctiveness), idealism, activism, globalism, ecology, self-actualization, and the importance of women. Are these individuals that Dr. Ray and Dr. Anderson speak of born with an agenda for motivating such social and spiritual progress in humans? Has our Creator mercifully encouraged the physical birth of advanced souls for the grand purpose of awakening in us what truly matters?

Many people believe that answer lies with what is called the "Indigo" and subsequent "Crystal" children; named for what is said to be the color of their auras or fields of energy. Believers say these children are being born to show us the way to make the transition to the next stage of our growth and evolution.

What are these Indigo and Crystal children like, and how could we tell if we know one (or more)? These children are said to be psychic, very sensitive, and forgiving individuals. They come into this world with a feeling of royalty or "deserving to be here". They are aware, sometimes painfully, of their differences with other "normal" children. It is said that Indigo children may not socialize unless it is with their own "kind". If they know of none they may turn inward and feel as though no one understands them. School life for these children can be difficult as they learn better with creative ways of instruction as opposed to rote learning. In fact they are often labeled as having ADD (attention deficit disorder) or ADHD (attention deficit hyperactivity disorder). The general agreement among believers is that Indigo children have been incarnating for the past hundred years with a major wave being born in the 1970s. Crystal children have only arrived within the last decade. They are said to be more easy-going and even-tempered when compared to Indigo children.

Similarities also exist with Indigo and Crystal children, and that which Dr. Elaine Aron calls the "highly sensitive" child. Recall that I mentioned Dr. Aron's studies of highly sensitive children in relation to the young who have some difficulty adapting to their physical world. In her book *The Highly Sensitive Child* Dr. Aron states that between 15 and 20 percent of all humanity can be defined as highly sensitive. And this has been the case throughout history, not just the past hundred years.

Highly sensitive individuals, says Dr. Aron, are the royal advisors, the writers, historians, philosophers, judges, artists, researchers, theologians, therapists, teachers, parents, and plain conscientious citizens. They bring nourishment to our society and inspire others to search for meaning. They are very intuitive and have a rich inner life. According to Dr. Aron, highly sensitive individuals experience spirituality deeply. They encounter intimate personal relationships with God, angels, saints, or spirit guides. They may perceive visions, synchronicities, and miracles. Is this sounding similar to the Indigo and Crystal children?

In abbreviated list form, note the similarities both in vocabulary and general meaning:

Indigo/Crystal Children	Highly Sensitive Children
*Are Psychic	*Are intuitive
* Have high sensitivity	* Are highly sensitive
*Have excessive amounts of energy; may appear to have short attention span.	*When over-aroused will be anxious, unfocused, and excitable.
*Can present as having Attention Deficit Disorder.	*Can present as having Attention Deficit Disorder.
*Require emotionally stable adults around him/her.	* Do best when treated with high responsiveness from adults who are not emotionally stressed.
* Have preferred ways of learning; learn best from an exploratory level.	* Learn best in an environment that is neither overstimulated nor overcrowded. Using creativity is highly effective.
*Are very compassionate. Have many fears such as death and loss of loved ones.	*Become truly upset by another's suffering. Feel things deeply.
*Do best with loving discipline, and open displays of love without hitting or using abusive language.	*Learn better from gentle correction than strong punishment.

Sources: *The Indigo Children. The New Kids Have Arrived.* By Lee Carroll & Jan Tober. *The Highly Sensitive Child. Helping Our Children Thrive When the World Overwhelms Them.* By Elaine N. Aron, Ph.D.

While researching the phenomenon of high sensitivity Dr. Aron learned what the great psychologist Carl Jung wrote almost half a century ago about people who were the "introverted and intuitive types". He claimed they are "educators and promoters of culture…their life teaches the other possibility, the interior life which is so painfully wanting in our society". Furthermore he said they are naturally more influenced by their unconscious, which gives them information of the "utmost importance", a "prophetic foresight".

I tend to agree with Dr. Jung and Dr. Aron's observation, in that they believe HSC have been around throughout history. Like them I also believe that these children were likely the ones who grew to inspire humanity's progress by becoming the great philosophers, writers, historians, theologians, judges, and artists of our past. And today they are the healthcare professionals, educators, research scientists, artists, musicians, and published authors who approach their work with an inner directedness and deep compassion for others. A "Cultural Creative", if you will.

Perhaps it is now more a question of numbers; an increase in the cited 15-20% of sensitive souls being born at this time who will in fact promote much needed change for our world. Visionaries and futurists have anticipated this occurrence for almost three decades. Has the time finally come when the vast majority will change the way they perceive reality? Looking at the current state of affairs it certainly seems humanity needs more than a nudge toward progression. We need a total overhaul of consciousness.

I, myself, was a highly sensitive child who is now a person who can be labeled a "Cultural Creative". Though I am not implying that I will be "great" in anything, I have always been highly intuitive and have known since my pre-school years that I wanted to help others in some capacity. I have a rich inner life and a strong dislike of the heavy emphasis placed on materialism in this society. Having an exceptionally turbulent childhood, including only completing the highest grade of fifth, I survived largely because of having the ability to access my intuition. I avoided school from the age of ten through sixteen because of the difficulty I had relating to my peers, as I believed they simply did not understand me. At the age of sixteen I took the general equivalency diploma exam and scored high enough to enter a senior college, despite having only completed fifth grade. I immediately enrolled in college, graduated with honors and dove into the social services field. After helping those with mental illness and substance abuse problems for a decade and becoming a mother, I realized my passions were being drawn to the miracle of new life. It then became a spiritual quest which led me to where I am at this point of my life. A maternal/child health nurse passionately trying to inspire people to view new life in a way which speaks to the very core of their soul. Something within my being propelled me to write this book, despite never having anything published in my name. It was not for the want of money or recognition. Like many other authors, this book was born of the desire to express what was emerging in my soul. An articulation of sheer reverence for what I consider to be the most beautiful and hopeful offering from our Creator: the birth of a child.

So whether we call them Indigo, Crystal, highly sensitive children (HSC), or budding Cultural Creatives, one thing we can all agree upon is that these particular qualities in a child undoubtedly make us pause. They have forced adults to look at things differently from the way we care for them at home, to the way they are educated or otherwise treated outside the home. They offer many gifts to humanity. If truly understood, I believe these children can promote reform of systems which no longer serve the expansion of spirit on all levels. The future awaits the grace of their presence. I hope the world takes heed.

But what is more important is the potential of *each and every child*. From the moment they are conceived know that they indeed arrive with universal purpose. Nurture a child's unique soul along with his mind and body, and watch as his full potential is unleashed. Be mindful that they are not extensions of the parent, but an entirely distinct entity. Encourage trueness to themselves that opens a realm of boundless possibilities, unobscured by insecurities, illusions, or fear. For nothing else can promote such health, sense of well-being, and fulfillment for our children as the accomplishment of aligning the brilliance of their soul with the logic of their mind and endurance of their body.

As your child grows, study his strengths and weaknesses and then help him choose a career path that will serve the power of his spirit. If you need assistance with guiding your older child's choice of career there are several excellent books designed to counsel based upon an individual's unique traits. One I like is *Do What You Are* By Paul D. Tieger and Barbara Barron-Tieger, but there are other fine works available. Many young adults make the mistake of getting caught up in a career path that is wrong for them. One which does not make use of their innate capacities, or works against the intricacies of their nature. How many times have you heard of a young person who went to college for a specific vocation only to find out after graduation she hates the job entailed? Sadly it happens all too often. And many do not get a second chance to pursue their true calling.

But the majority of children are amazingly resilient and often grow to find their purpose despite obstacles in their path. For it is the journey that matters most in terms of inner growth.

So the next time you see an infant, marvel at his courage for joining the rest of us. Then if you are like me, follow it with a "thank you" for making the world a more hopeful place to live in. As it is the journey of each child that brings the power of love and the promise of change… for you, for me, for all creation.

Resources

www.AskDrSears.com
This is Dr. William Sears and his family's website. It offers wonderfully heartfelt and effective guidance from a pediatrician who has authored numerous baby books, all of which are highly recommended.

www.IntuitiveNurturing.com
My website that contains information and articles on pregnancy, childbirth and childrearing based on my style of blending science and spirituality.

www.DONA.org
Website of Doulas of North America. Provides valuable information regarding the services of a doula as well as a directory available to find one in your area.

www.ACNM.com
American College of Nurse Midwives website. It offers information about midwifery practice and a directory to help you find a practitioner in your area.

www.LaLecheLeague.org
Website of La Leche League, the international organization of breastfeeding support that provides education and encouragement to women who wish to breastfeed their children.

www.attachmentparenting.org
Lovely website devoted to peaceful parenting. It provides helpful articles and information on bonding/attachment, co-sleeping, discipline, and breastfeeding.

www.Myss.com
Website of Caroline Myss, renowned author and medical intuitive. This website details the chakras in a spectacular interactive display. Very informative. Her books are excellent as well.

www.JudithOrloff.com
Website of Dr. Judith Orloff, psychiatrist, author, and medical intuitive. She offers helpful guidance in her numerous articles on health and spirituality and how to recognize your own intuition. I highly recommend her work.

ABOUT THE AUTHOR

Christine Ramos is a Registered Professional Nurse, Certified Childbirth Educator, and Certified Doula. Prior to becoming a nurse, she worked in the mental health field with the mentally disabled and substance abusers as a counselor, then later as an administrator of housing. She has earned two baccalaureate degrees, the first in Community Health Education from York College, City University of New York and the other in Nursing from State University New York at Stony Brook.

Being an intuitive, Christine has always been naturally drawn to matters of the soul. Since she was a teenager, she has studied spirituality and Eastern thought on well-being in an attempt to make sense of her extrasensory awareness. Becoming pregnant with her first child is what prompted Christine to change careers as she became captivated with the profoundly spiritual experience of bringing new life into the world. Wanting to pursue a second career in nurse-midwifery, she quit her job as an administrator and went back to school. To spare her family any financial hardship, she earned her nursing degree in as little time as possible by completing the 69 college credits needed in one year. But, instead of continuing her education in midwifery, Christine found herself working as a maternity nurse in a large New York hospital. (She has also cared for patients with cardiac problems.)

Christine is married, has two sons and a daughter and lives in Long Island, New York. This book was written within the stolen moments of the three and half years following the birth of her third child. Currently, she provides private pregnancy and postpartum services, and writes articles for parenting publications and websites.

Christine invites you to share experiences, questions, or comments related to the topics of this book. Please contact her at Christine@IntuitiveNurturing.com. For detailed information, articles, and updates on Christine's work, please visit her website at www.IntuitiveNurturing.com.

Other Books Published
by
Ozark Mountain Publishing, Inc.

Conversations with Nostradamus, Volume I, II, III...............by Dolores Cannon
Jesus and the Essenes...by Dolores Cannon
They Walked with Jesus..by Dolores Cannon
Between Death and Life.. by Dolores Cannon
A Soul Remembers Hiroshima...by Dolores Cannon
Keepers of the Garden..by Dolores Cannon
The Legend of Starcrash...by Dolores Cannon
Legacy from the Stars...by Dolores Cannon
The Custodians...by Dolores Cannon
The Convoluted Universe - Book One, Book Two..............by Dolores Cannon
Beauty and the Priest..by Reverend Patrick McNamara
I Have Lived Before...by Sture Lönnerstrand
The Forgotten Woman..by Arun & Sunanda Gandhi
Luck Doesn't Happen by Chance................................by Claire Doyle Beland
Mankind - Child of the Stars...........................by Max H. Flindt & Otto Binder
The Gnostic Papers..by John V. Panella
Past Life Memories As A Confederate Soldier.......................by James H. Kent
Holiday in Heaven..by Aron Abrahamsen
Is Jehovah An E.T.?..by Dorothy Leon
The Ultimate Dictionary of Dream Language.........................by Briceida Ryan
The Essenes - Children of the Light..............by Stuart Wilson & Joanna Prentis
Rebirth of the Oracle................................by Justine Alessi & M. E. McMillan
Reincarnation: The View from Eternity.....by O.T. Bonnett, M.D. & Greg Satre
The Divinity Factor..by Donald L. Hicks
What I Learned After Medical School ....by O.T. Bonnett, M.D.
A Journey Into Being.........................by Christine Ramos, RN, BSN, CCE, CD

For more information about any of the above titles, soon to be released
titles, or other items in our catalog, write or visit our website:

OZARK
MOUNTAIN
PUBLISHING

PO Box 754
Huntsville, AR 72740

www.ozarkmt.com
1-800-935-0045/479-738-2348 Wholesale Inquiries Welcome

NOTES

NOTES

NOTES

NOTES